ELVIS
THE #1 HITS

Patrick Humphries

Andrews McMeel
Publishing
Kansas City

First publication by Ebury Press in Great Britain in 2002

For information, write Andrews McMeel Publishing, an Andrews McMeel Universal company, 4520 Main Street, Kansas City, Missouri 64111.

ISBN: 0-7407-3803-8

Library of Congress Cataloging-in-Publication Data

Humphries, Patrick.
Elvis, the #1 hits : the secret history of the classics / Patrick Humphries
p. cm.
Includes bibliographical references.
ISBN 0-7407-3803-8
1. Presley, Elvis, 1935-1977. I. Title: Elvis, the number one hits. II. Title: Secret history of the classics. III. Title.

ML420.P96H86 2003
782.42166'092—dc21

2002045164

03 04 05 06 RDC 10 9 8 7 6 5 4 3 2 1

Created by Essential Books

All photographs are the property of Pictorial Press and Essential Books, all sleeves are from RCA records.

Author Acknowledgments

I'd like to thank Mal Peachey for asking me to write about Elvis for only the best reasons. While not directly consulted, Peter K. Hogan was a welcome ghost at this feast. Charlie Stanford at BMG helped with Elvis' plans for 2002, but couldn't get me that interview.

As ever, Sue Parr got me all shook up, and then ensured this wouldn't be returned to sender.

And remember: wise men say ... uh-hu-huh!

Patrick Humphries, London, May 2002

Contents

INTRODUCTION

BOB DYLAN SAID it best: 'Hearing Elvis for the first time was like busting out of jail!'

It is now nearly half a century since Elvis Presley first transfixed the world with his inimitable brand of rock'n'roll rebellion – but, even today, the shock of that awesome debut is still tangible.

It was Elvis who helped haul the black-and-white 50s' world out of its grim post-war limbo and ushered in the colourful second half of the 20th century. It was Elvis who single-handedly altered the look and the sound of the world we inhabit. It was Elvis who invented rock'n'roll. And all those who followed owed their inspiration to the man who was, and always will be, the King.

In the 25 years since his death, the shadow of Elvis has never ceased to loom large. But the question remains: which Elvis should we enshrine? The unknown teenager who took white country and western in one hand, black rhythm & blues in the other, and in the sweaty confines of Sun Studios fused them together to form rock'n'roll? The iconic, hip-swivelling Elvis whose unique look and peerless voice mesmerised the world during the mid-50s? The thirtysomething who snaked out of Hollywood in 1968, a leather-clad powerhouse keen to reclaim his crown? Or the white-jumpsuited Elvis who karate-kicked his way into Las Vegas during the 70s and raised the ante on live performance for ever?

There were contradictions too, at every stage of this extraordinary life. Elvis, the rebel who revered his mother; the stud who addressed every woman as 'Ma'am'; the boy steeped in the traditions and prejudices of the Deep South who brought black music to the white world; the trail-blazing musical pioneer who went on to record any musical pap they placed in front of him; the youthful revolutionary who delighted in hobnobbing with President Nixon; the consummate showman who allowed himself to be paraded around like a cheap fairground novelty.

The debate still rages as to which was the real Elvis – though of course, in the end, they're *all* Elvis. And that's what makes him the King.

EVEN IN DEATH, Elvis continues to haunt the popular imagination. You can pretty much take a degree in Elvisology in the 21st century; the imagined sightings still keep tabloid readers amused; Michael Jackson became his posthumous son-in-law. And then, of course, there are the songs – endlessly sung and played, recycled via radio, disc

'ELVIS PRESLEY'S DEATH DEPRIVES OUR COUNTRY OF A PART OF ITSELF, HIS MUSIC AND HIS PERSONALITY CHANGED THE FACE OF AMERICAN POPULAR CULTURE … ELVIS MAY BE GONE BUT HIS LEGEND WILL BE WITH US FOR A LONG TIME TO COME'

Jimmy Carter, President, 1977

and cyberspace. He is one of the most written-about men who has ever lived; and his image is so powerful that decades after his death the Elvis industry continues to go from strength to strength.

In the end though, it is the voice, above all, that lives on. From the very beginning as a bright and eager youngster capering around Sun Studios, excitedly hammering together two musical styles to create an unforgettable alloy all of his own, right up until the later years, spent booming out ballads in the massive auditoria that were his domain during the 70s – even during the frequently written-off Hollywood years – his voice never let him down.

Hearing those classic Elvis hits never fails to excite. But to grasp the full revolutionary impact of his music you need to put it in context: dig out a selection of soundtracks and compilation CDs of music from the early 50s, spend a little time wallowing in that cloying mixture of honeycomb, marshmallow and candy floss, and *then* put on 'Heartbreak Hotel' – you'll start to understand what a seismic effect Elvis had on the stultifying 50s.

In the beginning, they called him The Memphis Flash – and you can see why. Just take a look at those early photos: already Elvis stood out like an alien, isolated amidst the crew-cut conformity of those around him. In the 50s, when most Americans were still clinging to modest uniformity, everything about Elvis sneered individualism and rebellion. Within a few short years he would mesmerise the nation, but long before he swivelled the world upside down, he was already Elvis.

For all the shadows that would darken his later life, it remains true that as a young man Elvis illuminated our world. The rock'n'roll he forged back then may have started out as a home-grown novelty, barely heard outside of Memphis, Tennessee. But it is now a multi-billion dollar, pan-global industry. Without Elvis there would be no Beatles, no Rolling Stones, no REM; no Oasis, U2 or Strokes. It's fairly fanciful, but I have even heard it said that, 'without Elvis, the Berlin Wall wouldn't have come down!'

No other artist has made such an impact or left such an indelible impression on our times as Elvis. Hard to imagine, but the sneering, rebellious rocker, had he lived, would now be facing up to his 70th birthday. It is impossible from this perspective to imagine a world without Elvis – his voice booms out from radios and computers, the melodies of those songs ring in lifts and door chimes, the face stares from postage stamps and tea towels. From spaceships circling the further reaches of the Galaxy, the voice of Elvis echoes back. It is almost inconceivable that any single individual could have made such a mark.

ELVIS AARON PRESLEY was born on 8 January 1935, to Vernon and Gladys Presley, in Tupelo, Mississippi. Elvis was one of a pair of twins, but his brother Jesse was stillborn. Because he was the couple's only surviving child, Elvis was spoilt by his mother, Gladys. Father Vernon was a labourer, who in 1938–39 served eight months in Mississippi's infamous Parchman Farm Penitentiary for forging a cheque.

Each step of Elvis' young life has been painstakingly chronicled: the first public appearance, aged ten, singing 'Old Shep' at the Mississippi–Alabama Fair; his first guitar at the age of eleven; the Presley family's move to Memphis in 1948. At school, he veered between 'excellent' (at music) and straight Ds ('poor, but passing work' for Geography). On quitting Humes High and applying for a job, the teenager was already being noted as a 'rather flashily dressed "playboy" type'.

Afterhours too, the young Elvis stands out from the crowd – quite literally – one of the rare white faces to be seen in the audience for the gospel nights at Memphis' Ellis Auditorium. B.B. King also recalls seeing the teenage Elvis prowling the predominantly black blues clubs on Beale Street. But aside from his highly developed musical tastes, there was, as yet, little to suggest that the young Presley would ever amount to anything much. Chances were he was destined to live out his days in Memphis, driving trucks for the Crown Electric Company.

But all that changed one summer day during 1953, when Elvis Presley first entered Sam Phillips' Sun Studios, at 706 Union Avenue in Memphis. Keen to hear how his voice would sound on disc, the eighteen-year-old had decided to pay for himself to cut an acetate. After handing over his $4, Elvis began recording the two songs he had chosen: the Ink Spots' 1941 hit 'That's When Your Heartaches Begin' and the 1948 Pied Pipers ballad 'My Happiness'.

Sun Records' receptionist, Marion Keisker, was quietly impressed with the boy's voice and made a note to recommend him to label boss Sam Phillips. While she was filling out the paperwork, Marion had asked the boy who he thought he sounded like. In a voice that would soon reverberate around the world, Elvis Presley replied: 'I don't sound like nobody!'

SAM PHILLIPS WAS a big fish in a little pond. He had been cutting records at 706 Union since 1952, and among the earliest acts he recorded there were Rufus Thomas, Howlin' Wolf and Harmonica Frank. It was the only place in Memphis where black acts could go to get their music recorded. But Phillips recognised that in order to crack the really lucrative crossover market, he needed a marketable face – and in those days, in the Deep South, that meant a white face. 'If I could find a white man who had the Negro sound,' he said at the time, 'I could make a million dollars!'

Over the years that quote has caused much controversy. It has been alleged that Sam Phillips used the far more pejorative term '*nigger* sound', but those who knew him during the virtually apartheid years of late 40s' and early 50s' America never recall Phillips using that word. Indeed, Sam was known as a defiant defender of black music, in an era when such an attitude constituted a brave stand.

Elvis' own attitude toward race has also been questioned from time to time in recent years, with critics accusing him of stealing music away from its black originators. In fact, the young Elvis always acknowledged his debt to the musicians who inspired him; and – less directly – in almost every one of his recorded moments, the older Elvis shouted his debt and allegiance to black music.

It is worth remembering that Elvis began recording and espousing black music and musicians nearly a decade before Martin Luther King's historic march on Washington or Bob Dylan's songs protesting the iniquity of racism. And although his background may not have endowed him with a very sophisticated grasp of the issues, Elvis *was* sincerely proud of his musical heritage. His fondness for and appreciation of blues, R&B and gospel was instinctive, devout and genuine. All the more remarkable when you consider his upbringing in those days, and in that place.

WHEN MARION KEISKER played Elvis' first tentative recordings to Sam Phillips during 1953, Phillips immediately recognised an elusive something in the boy's performance – but it was to be a further year before he managed to isolate that distinctive quality and capture it on record.

Nobody really knew what to do with the boy. Musically, he drew deep from a rich well: in addition to the huge debt he owed to black music, Elvis revered crooners like Dean Martin and Mario Lanza, and the country sounds of Bill Monroe and Hank Williams. Phillips tried him out on everything – ballads, country, gospel, pop. He knew he had something , but he just couldn't seem to tap into it.

On one particular occasion, Elvis poured out his musical heart, singing a selection of current pop hits, Dean Martin ballads, gospel spirituals, R&B covers, anything to snatch Sam Phillips' attention. But it plainly wasn't working.

In desperation Sam puts Elvis in touch with Scotty Moore, a guitarist who sometimes helped him out on Sun sessions. Perhaps because of his innate shyness and musical uncertainty, Elvis still fails to unleash his pent-up musical frustration, despite a lot of encouragement from Scotty and his friend, bassist Bill Black. Until suddenly, sometime late in the afternoon of Monday 5 July 1954, it falls into place.

Elvis, Scotty and Bill are in the tiny studio at Sun; Sam Phillips is in the control booth. Tentative versions of 'I Love You Because' and 'Harbor Lights' are tried. It is swelteringly hot. The musicians fuel themselves with bottles of Coke. Then suddenly, from somewhere deep in the musical recesses of his memory, Elvis plucks Arthur 'Big Boy' Crudup's 'That's All Right, Mama', and starts hammering it out on his cheap guitar. The song began as a blues, but Elvis laid something special on it. Within a lick, Scotty and Bill have picked up on the groove – and in that one inspirational, improvised, incandescent moment, rock'n'roll was born.

Sam Phillips sticks his head out from the control room and roars, 'What are you doing?' Scotty admits that none of them has a clue. Sam tells them to do it again, and keep on doing it until they manage to replicate that fleeting sound. For the rest of that long, hot summer day the three youngsters do just that, until finally they nail their version of 'That's All Right, Mama'.

After that, things moved very fast and within a fortnight, the song would become Elvis Presley's first single. But the next day, 6 July 1954, Elvis, Scotty and Bill were back at Sun labouring under Sam Phillips' watchful eye. This time, the trio tackled 'Blue Moon Of Kentucky', one of the cornerstones of country music. But instead of Bill Monroe's stately waltz, the Memphis boys recut it as rock'n'roll. Scotty Moore remembered the quest as exciting and invigorating, but in the strictly hierarchical, white-dominated Memphis of the early 50s, they knew they were liable to be run out of town for their temerity.

'THAT'S ALL RIGHT, Mama', credited to 'Elvis Presley, Scotty and Bill', was released on 19 July 1954 with the catalogue number Sun Records 209. It wasn't the first rock'n'roll song: Jackie Brenston's 'Rocket 88' – featuring one Ike Turner – makes strong claim to that distinction. It wasn't even the first white rock'n'roll song – Bill Haley's 'Rock Around The Clock' had preceded it. Elvis didn't even invent the phrase 'rock'n'roll' – DJ Alan Freed deserves the credit for that. But what that teenage truck driver did do was to bring it all together, welding white country and black blues into an intriguing new sound.

It helped that Elvis was also young and sexy – capable of swivelling his hips, curling his lip and flicking his hair in less time than it took the avuncular Bill Haley to check that his kiss-curl was in situ. Even his name was unusual – posters from the period advertised 'Alvis' or 'Ellis' while his surname became 'Pressley' or 'Prestly'. But at least

Billboard, in their first mention of the phenomenon, managed to spell his name right – singling him out on that first seismic Sun single as 'a potent new chanter who can sock over a tune for either the country or r&b markets ... a strong new talent'.

So out they went, Elvis, Scotty and Bill, in a battered old Cadillac, criss-crossing the Deep South to promote each new release. It was, lest we forget, nearly half a century ago. Hank Williams was barely cold in the ground; Robert Allen Zimmerman had just been barmitzvahed; and it would be three years before John Lennon even met Paul McCartney.

The only way for the Memphis trio to really get their music across was to play it live in front of audiences, who were growing increasingly hysterical. The rest of 1954, and on throughout 1955, was spent making personal appearances and doing sporadic radio slots. And in between those gruelling one-night stands, the trio would head back to Memphis and cut further sides for Sam Phillips.

What Elvis achieved with the help of Scotty Moore, Bill Black and Sam Phillips, dwarfed everything that had gone before and shadowed everything that came after. The five singles Elvis Presley cut for Sun are landmarks, each offering up a heady mixture of rhythm & blues and country and western. The dark powerhouse of 'Mystery Train'; the freewheeling 'I'm Left, You're Right, She's Gone'; the exuberant 'Good Rockin' Tonight' – and the rest, together laid the very foundations of rock'n'roll.

Prior to signing with RCA, however, Elvis Presley was just a blip. He remained almost exclusively a regional phenomenon, the kid nurtured by Sam Phillips and championed by Memphis DJ Dewey Phillips. Scotty Moore tried managing the boy for a while – and soon realised that his strengths were as a guitarist. Memphis DJ Bob Neal then took his 15%, but by the middle of 1955 it was apparent that Elvis had already outgrown Sun and the South.

His appeal was spreading, but it was a slow build. It would take the double-whammy of a new manager, Colonel Tom Parker, and a contract with the mighty RCA Victor Records to transform the shy kid who could set any Saturday night hop alight into an international phenomenon.

Parker was a canny businessman who already looked after country stars Hank Snow and Eddy Arnold and, when his eye lighted on the new boy, Tom Parker paid Sam Phillips $35,000 for Elvis. To his credit, Sam Phillips has never evinced any bitterness over a deal that many regard as the worst since the Indians sold Manhattan Island for $20.

His new manager may have made him a star, but Elvis never forgot Sun Studios. Phillips had given him the template for his singular sound and at Elvis' early sessions for RCA in Nashville and New York, much time was spent trying to recapture that elusive 'Sun sound'. Elvis would return to Sun, and he was not the only one to make the pilgrimage. In 1988, when they were the biggest band on the planet, U2 moved into 706 Union Avenue to record, hoping to recreate some of that magic for themselves.

MUCH HAS BEEN written by critics battling for the soul of Elvis Presley, about the sense of betrayal, the cheap Hollywood compromises, the bloated caricature who reigned in Las Vegas, and the hollowness at the heart of the American Dream. But one thing that cannot be denied is the rare and instinctive talent of the young Elvis.

You might argue that there were half a hundred hillbilly cats strutting their stuff around the Deep South in the long evening of the Eisenhower presidency who *could* have done it. But the fact remains: it was a teenager called Elvis Presley who actually did do it. And you can hear just *how* he did it in December 1954, when Elvis, Scotty and Bill were cutting 'Milkcow Blues Boogie'.

'Hold on fellas,' snaps Elvis after a stilted eight-bar blues opening, 'that don't *move* me, let's get real, real gone ...' And that's just what they did – which is why the records Elvis cut in that tiny, sweaty studio remain unique, and why the music he made during his sixteen-month stint at Sun changed everything.

In 1975, Roy Carr of *New Musical Express* collected together all the available sides Elvis cut for Sun. *Elvis: The Sun Sessions* came out at a time when rock was floundering in the deep topographic oceans of progression. It was twenty years since Elvis had first gone out on a limb, but in the smoky back rooms of pubs around London, a number of bands were showing their determination to take rock back to its roots. Pub rock didn't register much in record sales, but it put the edge back on rock'n'roll, and kicked the door wide open for punk.

The spirit of that 70s' rebellion found echo in the music Elvis had created all those years before. Hearing the King's Sun records all gathered together was revelatory. It reminded those who cared, just how *much* Elvis had mattered – and still did.

As Roy Carr wrote in his sleevenotes: 'Though everyone from The Beatles right on through to Creedence and Dylan have, at one time or another, attempted to pay homage to the Sun sound, no one has successfully managed to recreate either the innocence or the stark and primal essence of these tapes. And I very much doubt if anyone ever will … These are rock'n'roll's definitive recordings.'

Something sparked in Elvis Presley during that hot July afternoon in 1954. Like a lightning conductor he was struck by the sudden possibility of change, of metamorphosis, of revolution. The moment was decisive, instinctive, electrifying – and from that single spontaneous session, Elvis went on to produce some of the most exhilarating and influential popular music of the twentieth century.

You may quibble over the direction of his later career, but you cannot help but love what Elvis was at the very beginning, before the world went mad. Just listen to the way he talks through 'I Love You Because', the very first song he recorded at his first professional studio session. Hear the clumsy sincerity, the naive delight. Hear him talk of the future that stretches bright ahead. Hear the potential, the sheer naked *promise* of it.

HEARTBREAK HOTEL

Written by Mae Boren Axton, Tommy Durden, Elvis Presley

Recorded 10 January 1956 at RCA Studios, Nashville

Guitar: Scotty Moore, Chet Atkins, Elvis Presley
Bass: Bill Black
Drums: D.J. Fontana
Piano: Floyd Cramer
Vocals: Gordon Stoker, Ben and Brock Speer

Released 27 January 1956

Heartbreak Hotel

It was as if the world had been holding its breath and waiting for Elvis Presley.

Too often calendar years are described as 'seismic', but 1956 – the year that marked Elvis Presley's first major record release – really did see the world teetering on the brink of change.

On the global stage, Britain's role as a world power was undermined by the public humiliation of the Suez Crisis – an event that ended the premiership of Anthony Eden and saw the biggest public demonstrations in London since the East End had taken to the streets to battle Mosley's Blackshirts twenty years before. In the East, Kruschev's speech denouncing Stalin's crimes at the party congress marked the first crack in the façade of the stony Soviet state, but neighbouring Hungary made a grave mistake when it took the Soviet premier's speech as a green light signifying that the nightmare years of Stalin's iron-fisted rule had passed. Before long Russian tanks had rolled across the border, crushing the nascent rebellion beneath their tracks. The Cold War returned to its familiar icy stasis, while in Cuba, the guerrilla forces of Fidel Castro waged war against the corrupt regime of President Batista.

In the theatre, John Osborne's *Look Back In Anger* delivered the first thrust against the conservative traditions of British stage drama, while *My Fair Lady* opened on Broadway, and was hailed as the best musical ever. Television was still a relative newcomer, but British viewers were now luxuriating in the choice of not one but two television channels, while across Europe nations united to watch the first Eurovision Song Contest.

In America, President Dwight D. Eisenhower comfortably beat Democrat Adlai Stevenson in the race for the White House – proving that the United States was in no mood for change just yet. The nation was happy enjoying its burgeoning baby boom and the country's status as a consumer

L-R: Scotty Moore, Elvis and Bill Black give it too much.

paradise. But Stevenson's defeat made one young Democratic senator, by the name of John F. Kennedy, determined to run for President in 1960. Way down in Alabama, a weary black maid called Rosa Parkes refused to give up her seat on a Montgomery bus to a white passenger and inadvertently triggered the fight for Civil Rights. The movement, spearheaded by the Reverend Martin Luther King, soon grew into a nationwide campaign that would divide America for the next decade. In contrast, few readers of American newspapers even bothered with the news that 1956 also saw the last French troops leaving Vietnam.

This was the world into which Elvis Presley hurtled at the very beginning of 1956.

Heartbreak Hotel

‘BLACKS DIDN’T HAVE THE AIRWAVES. ELVIS HAD. HE DELIVERED WHAT HE OBTAINED BEAUTIFULLY’ Chuck Berry

The first song Elvis cut on 10 January 1956 at his debut session for RCA was Ray Charles’ ‘I Got A Woman’. Later that day at the company’s Nashville Studio, after only seven takes, he nailed another song – one that had been pitched to him the previous year and that would be released within weeks as his debut single on RCA, the label he would remain with for the rest of his life. The song was ‘Heartbreak Hotel’.

It was while performing in Jacksonville, Florida in 1955 that Elvis had met schoolteacher and sometime songwriter Mae Boren Axton, who convinced him that she could write him his first million-seller. Later that year, Mae’s songwriting partner Tommy Durden showed her a newspaper story in the *Miami Herald* about an unknown suicide whose one-line epitaph read simply, ‘I walk a lonely street.’ Twenty minutes later ‘Heartbreak Hotel’ came into the world.

A few weeks later Mae Axton played the demo to Elvis, who agreed to record it. Mae then pitched the song to Colonel Parker who also agreed to take it, but only on the condition that his boy be given a one-third composer credit and royalty.

Mae consented, and then drifted out of the Elvis story – except for the postscript that her son, Hoyt Axton, also went on to enjoy a successful career writing songs, including ‘Never Been To Spain’, which Elvis recorded in 1972.

The brief at RCA’s Nashville Studio in January 1956 was to replicate the sound Sam Phillips had conjured up in Memphis. All the same ingredients were there, but this time there was enormous pressure on the musicians to try and recapture something that had been magical, but momentary, only months before.

At Sun Records it had all been fun. For Elvis, goofing around on his beat-up acoustic guitar came as a welcome relief from his job as a truck driver. Seasoned Sun veterans Scotty Moore and Bill Black joined in spontaneously, although not really sure how or what they were doing – or why they were doing it. Meanwhile, in the control room, Sam Phillips rocked with delight, and tried to catch that fleeting moment on tape. Now, in Nashville, things were a lot more serious: there was a whole heap of speculation and interest – not to mention money – riding on the 21-year-old Presley's shoulders.

Elvis celebrates signing with RCA by beating out a rhythm, 1955.

To capitalise on the growing media interest in Elvis, RCA rushed out 'Heartbreak Hotel' in late January 1956. *Billboard* called it: 'a strong blues item wrapped up in his usual powerful style and a great beat'. The review may have held Elvis' attention briefly, but he was too busy – touring Texas and Louisiana, before flying to New York to record – to rest on his laurels for long.

The day after 'Heartbreak Hotel' was released, Elvis made his national TV debut on *Stage Show*, but curiously didn't perform his new single. It was to be a month before 'Heartbreak Hotel' entered the American charts, at No.68 on 3 March 1956; and it took a further two months for the record – Elvis' first release on a major record label – to make it all the way. 'Heartbreak Hotel' finally reached No.1, deposing Les Baxter's 'The Poor People Of Paris', on 5 May 1956.

In Britain, 'Heartbreak Hotel' emerged as a 78rpm recording on His Master's Voice, the label that had earlier declined the option to release any of Elvis' Sun singles; and when *New Musical Express* reviewed the record, credited to 'Elvis Presley with rhythm accompaniment', it lamented: 'If you appreciate good singing, I don't suppose you'll manage to hear this disc all through'.

The CD sleeve of the 1996 release of the classic 1956 recordings.

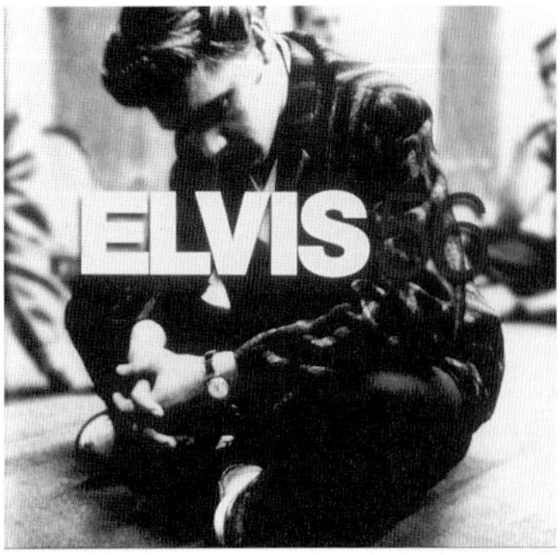

Not for the first time, *NME*'s comments apparently fell on deaf ears and Elvis Presley made his UK chart debut on 12 May 1956, when 'Heartbreak Hotel' entered the Hit Parade at No.15. Other chart positions that week were occupied by Winifred Atwell, David Whitfield, Dean Martin, Edmund Hockridge and Alma Cogan. 'Heartbreak Hotel' eventually reached No.2 in the UK, kept off the top slot by Ronnie Hilton's 'No Other Love'; but although Elvis failed to make it to No.1 on this occasion, 'Heartbreak Hotel' was without doubt the fusillade that launched the rock'n'roll rebellion in Britain.

Heartbreak Hotel

Bill Haley may have rocked around the clock a little earlier, but time was already telling on the former country and western singer – Haley was just too chubby, too cosy, to be a real teenage idol. 'Heartbreak Hotel' on the other hand, was an urgent and sensual clarion call that reached out to a whole generation. Youngsters, chafing against the idea of being little more than pint-sized versions of their parents, found little to identify with in the other popular music of the time; but when Elvis took that walk down lonely street to 'Heartbreak Hotel' he spoke straight to the hearts of a previously silent, disenfranchised generation.

Right from the beginning, the record grabbed listeners by the throat: Scotty Moore's guitar raged and rocked; Elvis' vocal swaggered, but also reached out with the longing of those lyrics. 'Heartbreak Hotel' was full of alienation, loneliness and despair.

And the kids absolutely loved it. In their millions.

If there had been a rock'n'roll hero previously, it was James Dean, who died in a car crash three months before Elvis recorded 'Heartbreak Hotel'. The actor only lived to see one of his three films released, but in the tragic aftermath of his death, the cult of James Dean had flourished. Youngsters on both sides of the Atlantic found solace in James Dean's moody, misunderstood martyr in *Rebel Without A Cause*, but they knew that after *Giant* there would be no more Dean films. And looking around for another idol, they happened upon that record, that voice, that man ... The newly identified teenagers of the 50s had, at last, found their role model.

For years afterwards, 'Heartbreak Hotel' defined Elvis Presley – the echo-soaked voice, the plaintive lament of the singer down at the end of lonely street, the potent sexual promise offered to broken-hearted lovers. But although Elvis had made the song his own, his success sparked covers from a bewildering array of other artists, including Roger Miller, Lawrence Welk, Albert King, Neil Diamond, Bert Jansch, Frijid Pink, Billy Joel, The Chieftains, Willie Nelson, The Cramps, Michael Jackson, Phil Ochs and John Cale.

'Heartbreak Hotel' marked the beginning for Elvis Presley, but the success of that record and its singer also marked the end of an era for the popular music industry. And, in turn, for the wider world outside.

The A–Z of Elvis

A is for Aaron

Elvis' middle name has been the subject of much speculation and interpretation since his death. His birth certificate, filled out by his father Vernon, spells it with one A; a compilation album released in 1980 bore the title Elvis Aron Presley. Yet the correct spelling was with two As – witness the headstone on his grave. The discrepancy in the spelling has prompted speculation that Elvis was of Jewish descent and of Welsh ancestry, Aron being the Welsh variation on the spelling (see A–Z, W is for Welsh). In truth it's likely that the poorly educated Vernon didn't know how to spell any word that began with two As, and had probably never heard of no Aardvark, either. On being sent to fill out official forms by his wife Gladys, he was probably instructed verbally what the boy's name would be and guessed at the spelling. Later in life Elvis would take his momma's side and spell his middle name with two As. His stillborn twin Jesse Garon had just the one A in his middle name. Of course, Elvis Is Alive conspirators believe that the two As on the headstone prove beyond doubt that it isn't the King in the grave. Probably some damned Aardvark.

I WANT YOU, I NEED YOU, I LOVE YOU

Written by Maurice Mysels, Ira Kosloff

Recorded 14 April 1956 at RCA Studios, Nashville

Guitar: Scotty Moore, Chet Atkins, Elvis Presley
Bass: Bill Black
Drums: D.J. Fontana
Piano: Marvin Hughes
Vocals: Gordon Stoker, Ben and Brock Speer

Released 4 May 1956

There have been a few rock'n'roll deaths caused by aeroplane disasters, most notably those of Buddy Holly, The Big Bopper and Ritchie Valens in February 1959. But if, on Friday 13 April 1956 the light aircraft carrying Elvis from Memphis to Nashville had suffered complete engine shutdown, rather than only partial failure, his death would have been that decade's defining disaster. The landing in Nashville was shaky, to say the least, which probably accounts for the fact that 'I Want You, I Need You, I Love You' was the only song recorded the day after. It was a scary enough incident to put Elvis off flying for a while, anyway.

The narrowly-avoided plane crash may have contributed to the discernable shakey quality to Elvis' voice the next day. To the unaware listener, there is a tremor of longing and barely concealed lust in Elvis' voice as he intones the lyric by Maurice Mysels, which is not just due to the excess of reverb on the recording. Whether the tremulous quality is caused by Elvis' still-knocking knees or not, the impression is one of a man quaking with desire. Essentially the lyric (by a jobbing pair of songwriters who contributed to the canon of Perry Como, among others) is standard boy-meets-girl, boy-falls-for-girl fare. The singer lets slip a mask of detached masculinity, the object of his desire proving to him that he was wrong to think that he'd never fall in love. However, as Elvis sings it, 'I Want You, I Need You, I Love You' is a hormone-fuelled primal scream of sexual fervour. Building from an

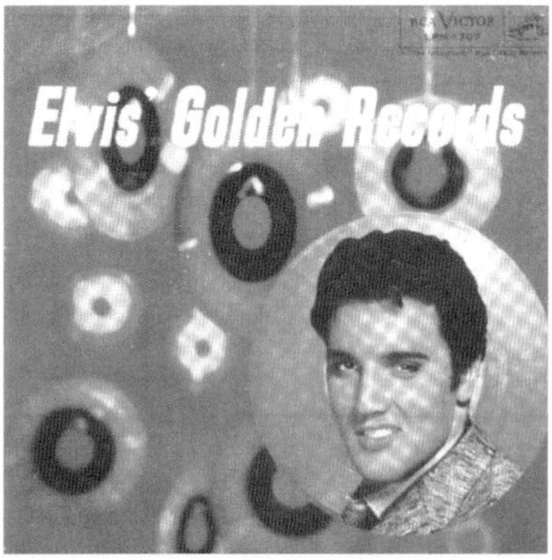

The CD sleeve of the first *Elvis' Golden Records* compilation which contains 'I Want You, I Need You, I Love You'.

'IF ANY INDIVIDUAL OF OUR TIME CAN BE SAID TO HAVE CHANGED THE WORLD, ELVIS PRESLEY IS THE ONE'

Greil Marcus, rock author

almost wan beginning as Scotty's guitar strums a shrill intro while the Speers brothers and Gordon Stoker provide a wordless doo-wop style backing, Elvis gets more insistent with each chorus that passes that he Wants, he Needs, he LOVES you.

The song provides possibly the first echo-sodden 'Ah-Ah' that was so beloved of Cliff Richard (and brilliantly copied by him, too). The barely pronounced, flattened Deep South 'Ah' (read as 'I') is almost a hiccup, a faltering adolescent gasp perched precariously between a pre-teen falsetto and deep masculine bass. It's one of the defining vocal tricks of the 50s' Elvis and had become a rock'n'roll cliché by the time the single had sold its millionth copy.

'I Want You, I Need You, I Love You' also bears the somewhat dubious distinction of being the famous 'other song'. As everyone knows, Elvis' performance of 'Hound Dog' on *The Milton Berle Show* of 5 June 1956 caused a storm of protest when he suggestively rotated his hips in time to the song (see the entry for 'Hound Dog', page 26). However, that protest was undoubtedly over-stoked by his more than suggestive rendition of 'I Want You …', a rendition that helped to sell the single. Moreover, Elvis' 1 July performance on *The Steve Allen Show* is famous for the filming of his duet with a bassett hound (with Elvis dressed in top hat and tails) as he sang 'Hound Dog', but as the song was not to be released as a single until later that month, it was 'I Want You …', performed on the same night, that shifted the units for him.

DON'T BE CRUEL

Written by Otis Blackwell, Elvis Presley

Recorded 2 July 1956 at RCA Studios, New York

Guitar: Scotty Moore, Elvis Presley
Bass: Bill Black
Drums: D.J. Fontana
Piano: Shorty Long
Vocals: The Jordanaires

Released 13 July 1956

Don't Be Cruel

After playing a solid week of concerts around the Deep South, Elvis travelled by train to New York to appear on TV's *Steve Allen Show*. He performed his current hit 'I Want You, I Need You, I Love You' – but was under strict instructions not to dance while he sang. The day after the show, Elvis made his first and only visit to his new label's New York studios, where he would record one of his best-loved hits.

Young Americans may still have gone out to buy 78rpm records and kept their ears glued to the popular new transistor radios, but in the mid-50s it was the power of television that really moved them. The most influential man on American television was the granite-faced Ed Sullivan, who was shocked by what he had seen of Elvis Presley. But Sullivan knew what made good television. Ironically though, when Elvis appeared on *The Ed Sullivan Show* for the first time in September 1956, the host was in hospital and his place was taken by the actor Charles Laughton. Elvis was, of course, a sensation.

Having attracted an audience of over 50 million viewers with his first appearance, it was inevitable that Elvis would be invited back. In January 1957 Sullivan himself hosted the show, introducing Elvis to the audience as 'a real decent, fine boy' – but just to be sure not to cause offence they took the precaution of filming Elvis only from the waist up.

By the summer of 1956, Elvis was the biggest entertainment phenomenon that the nation had ever seen. Frank Sinatra attracted screaming bobbysoxers a decade earlier but, by the mid-50s, as the post-war baby-boomers began to hit the market place with ready money, the teenager was born.

Everywhere he went, Elvis was greeted by increasingly large numbers of hysterical, screaming fans. In Elvis they saw the personification of everything their parents had warned them against – and they loved it. Though Little Richard, Chuck Berry and Fats Domino were also making their mark on the

Elvis, Scotty and Bill in action, early 1950s.

rock'n'roll charts, such was the prejudice of the period that theirs were still seen as 'race records'. Elvis, for all his sexual menace, was at least white.

A systematic re-release of all Elvis' Sun singles kept him buoyant in the charts throughout 1956, but although he was making a mark, RCA were still wary of their new signing. A&R man Steve Sholes was the executive who had gone out on a limb the previous year and authorised the $35,000 expenditure – beating off Atlantic Records' Ahmet Ertegun – but neither he nor RCA were convinced that Elvis Presley had legs. Alfred Wertheimer, who spent much of the crucial year of 1956 photographing Elvis – on the road, off-duty and in the studio – recalled RCA advising him to work in black and white, as it was cheaper than colour and Elvis may not be around for long.

Any doubts about Elvis' longevity finally came to an end with the success of his third RCA single. 'Don't Be Cruel' came to Elvis from New York-born songwriter Otis Blackwell, who had already written 'Great Balls Of Fire' for Jerry Lee Lewis and Peggy Lee's 'Fever'. As was to become customary, Colonel Parker insisted that Elvis be credited as co-writer; Blackwell was sensible enough to realise that even 50% of an Elvis Presley record was worth having.

He may not have had anything to do with the actual writing, but nevertheless 'Don't Be Cruel' became an Elvis song by sheer dint of his interpretive ability. The record was also another example of how much care Elvis took in the recording process: during the seven-hour session that day, Elvis cut just three tracks, and he lingered over each – 'Don't Be Cruel' took 28 takes before it was nailed to his satisfaction.

Elvis shaking hands with RCA A&R man Steve Sholes, 1955.

'Don't Be Cruel' – the flipside of 'Hound Dog' – eventually reached No.1 on the *Billboard* chart in September 1956, but equally gratifying for Elvis was the knowledge that he had finally pacified at least one critic of his RCA recordings. Sam Phillips, though content with the financial side of the deal, was disappointed by the records Elvis had been making since his departure from Sun Records. But 'Don't Be Cruel' changed all that: 'I thought, they have finally found this man's ability,' Phillips recalled in the booklet accompanying *The Essential 50s Masters*. 'The rhythm was right, and it was moving along just right, it had that absolute spontaneity, and yet Elvis still had command, which I always wanted him to have when he was with me.'

'Don't Be Cruel' was also notable as the first single on which Elvis recorded with The Jordanaires – the vocal quartet who went on to work closely with him for many years and sang on many of his biggest hits. Soon after the publication of Albert Goldman's bile-filled 1981 biography of Elvis, Gordon Stoker of The Jordanaires shook his head at the savagery of Goldman's attack, baffled by the book's depiction of a man he simply did not recognise. The Jordanaires worked with Elvis on and off for a dozen years, and spent time with him both professionally and socially. Stoker remembered a disciplined musician and a gentle man. The Elvis he recalled was an instinctive musician, his senses well-honed and truly appreciative of the rich well of black culture on which he drew so deeply. Gordon Stoker's Elvis was far removed from the racist monster unleashed by Albert Goldman.

Some later critics have accused 'Don't Be Cruel' of demonstrating a smoother, more diluted side of Elvis, but it remains a firm popular favourite that has been covered by a number of other acts, including Cheap Trick, Neil Diamond, Jerry Lee Lewis, James Last and The Judds.

Colonel Parker's plan to keep his boy in the public eye in order to help promote 'Don't Be Cruel' included booking him in for a month-long stint in Las Vegas. But the residency was not a success and for the first time in 18 months the momentum faltered. Quite simply, Elvis bombed. His sexually charged performance was seriously at odds with the middle-aged gamblers of middle America and the engagement was terminated after just two weeks.

One positive thing did emerge from that Las Vegas engagement, however. Crossing the lobby of the New Frontier Hotel one day, Elvis heard Freddie Bell & The Bellboys performing. The group were larking around on a version of a Big Mama Thornton blues that mightily impressed Elvis and he made a mental note to do something about it.

The A–Z of Elvis

B is for Black Leather

When British former boy band crooner Robbie Williams appeared live on the prestigious business awards ceremony The Brits in 2000, he ironically wore a black leather suit that was closely modelled on the same two-piece Elvis had worn for his 1968 TV comeback special. That Williams sang a duet with Tom Jones while wearing the black leather suit added to the irony, of course (or not). Williams was not the first, nor shall he be the last, minor pop star to don a replica comeback special suit in order to persuade people that he is, in some way, associated with Elvis. Former Teardrop Explodes singer Julian Cope had worn something similar during a solo tour in 1987. In the early 70s glam rock oddity Alvin Stardust grossly overdid the Elvis homage while miming his 'Coo-Coo-Cha-Coo' hit by introducing flares and adding a cheap, gaudy, over-sized ring worn over backless leather gloves. Elvis' suit, in fact, was made by his personal costume designer Bill Belew (see J is for Jumpsuit) who 'had no recollection of Elvis wearing leather as a performer and liked the idea of the mystique of leather'. Belew had just finished designing costumes for Petula Clark when he got the gig designing for the comeback special. Elvis must have liked the cut of his leather, because he employed Bill thenceforth. The only previous sighting of the King in black leather was in the 1964 movie *Roustabout.*

HOUND DOG

Written by Jerry Leiber and Mike Stoller

Recorded 2 July 1956 at RCA Studios, New York

Guitar: Scotty Moore, Elvis Presley
Bass: Bill Black
Drums: D.J. Fontana
Piano: Shorty Long
Vocals: The Jordanaires

Released 13 July 1956

For many people 'Hound Dog' was, and still is, *the* Elvis single. Its impact at the time was nothing short of electrifying.

Where the Elvis of 'Heartbreak Hotel' had come across as plaintive and full of longing, on 'Hound Dog' he sounded full of menace. There was something confrontational, almost dangerous, about the way Elvis relished the opening line. And it was a threat made all the more real by the controversy surrounding his recent television appearances. The sight of Elvis in full sneering, snake-like performance had sent shockwaves across America – a country that still took its opinions from the *Readers' Digest* and its entertainment courtesy of the virginal Doris Day.

Even now, nearly half a century on, 'Hound Dog' still sounds thrilling – the combination of Elvis' raucous vocal, Scotty Moore's electric guitar and D.J. Fontana's machine-gun drumming made sure of that. It may not have sounded the clarion call of Eddie Cochran's 'Summertime Blues', but to young and old alike, the symbolism was clear. Elvis was the harbinger of something wild, holding out a tantalising promise: entry to a club where the dress code was blue suede shoes and the password incomprehensible to anyone over twenty.

Songwriters Jerry Leiber and Mike Stoller began writing together in 1950 and had already seen their songs cut by leading figures on the R&B scene, including Little Esther, Johnny Otis and Big Mama Thornton. In fact, Big Mama Thornton's recording of 'Hound Dog' had already reached No.1 on the R&B chart by the time Elvis came to record it in 1956.

A British version of 'Heartbreak Hotel' 45rpm single. 'Blue Suede Shoes' is on the B-side.

Elvis' version of the song sprung to life one hot summer's day at RCA's New York studios – and despite being squeezed in between a round of increasingly hysterical live performances, radio interviews and television appearances, the session proved that Elvis had lost none of his painstaking enthusiasm for the recording process. 'Hound Dog' took 31 takes to get right to the singer's satisfaction – but even before he stepped into that studio, the song's notoriety was assured.

'Hound Dog' was destined from the start to become one of Elvis' most controversial singles. Performing it on *The Milton Berle Show* on 5 June 1956, a month before he recorded the song, Elvis' pelvic perambulations had shocked the millions of Americans who had tuned in for an evening of cosy variety with the much-loved Uncle Miltie. Along with The Beatles' 1964 appearance on *The Ed Sullivan Show*, Elvis' performance of 'Hound Dog' that night remains one of the most seismic rock'n'roll moments in television history.

The outrage was palpable – writing in the *Journal American*, Jack O'Brian was shocked by 'a display of primitive physical movement difficult to describe in terms suitable to a family newspaper!' America had never seen anything like it – Elvis was the all too physical embodiment of troubled, turbulent youth. Suddenly the phrase juvenile delinquency was on everyone's lips: in Britain, elaborately quiffed Teddy

The A–Z of Elvis

C is for Cosa Nostra

During Elvis' lifetime the Cosa Nostra, or Mafia, were an all-pervasive force in the entertainment business. They owned record companies, distribution chains, record stores, nightclubs, even performers' contracts. That they had no contact with the biggest star in rock'n'roll is highly unlikely. That the Colonel chose Las Vegas as the location for Elvis' big return to live performances in 1969 suggests that the Italian gentlemen who ran the city had some part in at least the third phase of the King's career. Elvis had performed in Vegas in April 1956 but had his residency cut short due to a lack of interest from the middle-aged audiences. At that point the Mafia may well have ignored Elvis, but by the beginning of the 60s they would have changed their mind about him. Which might account for the never-ending tours in the desert. The Colonel was apparently addicted to roulette and his losses must have been immense. He owed the casino bosses. Not that Elvis was likely to be aware of any such connections. He was probably even unaware of the fact that Luigi and Hugo, the writers of the hit single from *Blue Hawaii*, 'Can't Help Falling In Love', had been partners with a renowned Mafia henchman – Mo Levy – in ownership of Roulette Records. The FBI had described the company as providing a steady stream of income to the Genovese crime family and in 1988 Levy was convicted of conspiracy to commit extortion.

In the mid-1990s Elvis Presley Enterprises marketed a replica of the shirt the King had worn at his last day job before becoming a rock icon. Detail, above, from over the breast pocket of that shirt.

Boys prowled the still bomb-scarred streets, whilst in America, gangs (like those depicted in Marlon Brando's *The Wild One*) terrorised whole neighbourhoods. Elvis Presley was seen as the figurehead of seething teenage rebellion, a position only confirmed by his sensational appearance on *The Milton Berle Show*.

The shockwaves generated by Elvis' most recent TV appearance were still reverberating when Colonel Parker got his boy another TV slot to promote the new single, just days before its release. But the singer who appeared on *The Steve Allen Show* was a deliberately restrained and subdued presence – gone were the cocky flips and sexy smirks. Here instead was a smartly dressed Elvis, singing 'Hound Dog' in the direction of a nervous-looking Basset hound wearing a top hat.

A few months earlier in March 1956, the album *Elvis Presley* – released to demonstrate the variety and versatility of Presley's talent – had helped fuel the phenomenon that was now sweeping the nation. 'Elvis is the most popular protagonist of popular songs on the scene today,' the sleeve proclaimed, 'His style stands out vividly on records and in personal appearances and accounts for the universal popularity he has gained.'

It was all happening so fast. From the small-time hillbilly craze of just a few months before, Elvis had gone on to become the most talked-about person in the country. 'My daddy and I were laughing about it the other day,' Elvis reflected at the time. 'He looked at me and said, "What happened, El? The last thing I can remember is I was working in a can factory and you were driving a truck!"'

The reason Elvis quit his job at Crown Electric . . . live on stage circa 1955.

'I DON'T KNOW ANYONE OF MY AGE THAT DID NOT SING LIKE HIM, AT ONE TIME OR ANOTHER' Bob Dylan

LOVE ME TENDER

Written by Elvis Presley, Vera Matson

Recorded 24 August 1956 at Stage 1, 20th Century Fox Studios, Hollywood

Guitar: Vito Mumolo
Bass: Mike 'Myer' Rubin
Drums: Richard Cornell
Banjo: Luther Rountree
Accordion: Dom Frontieri
Vocals: Rad Robinson, Jon Dodson, Charles Prescott

Released: 28 September 1956

Love me Tender

Elvis had just turned 21 and his every gyration was making national news. With every record effortlessly climbing the charts and James Dean barely cold in his grave, it was inevitable that Hollywood would soon be calling.

Midway through 1956, it was too early to judge the full impact that rock'n'roll was to have; but Colonel Parker was already working on a long-term plan for his boy. Elvis had bombed in Las Vegas and his antics on television had caused critical heart failure, so his canny manager began the process of smoothing the rough edges off the Presley persona. At the time, all rock'n'roll singers claimed their ambition was to become 'an all-round entertainer'. None of them, or their managers, could really believe this rebellious teenage music would last, so a career in television, pantomime or cabaret seemed pretty appealing. With a bit of luck you might even land a role in a film. And if luck was really running with you, a proper film career could follow.

Elvis began his film career in a project called *The Reno Brothers*, a Civil War drama, but only after Colonel Parker had declined on his behalf the opportunity to star opposite Burt Lancaster and Katherine Hepburn in *The Rainmaker* – because, the Colonel reasoned, the script was too dramatic.

The Reno Brothers was soon re-titled *Love Me Tender*, thus cashing in on the theme song that had received a nice plug when Elvis sang it on *The Ed Sullivan Show* just prior to flying out to Hollywood to begin filming. On arrival, Elvis was disturbed to learn that the film's musical director, Ken Darby, unhappy with the calibre of Elvis' long-time backing musicians – Scotty Moore, Bill Black and D.J. Fontana, had decided to replace them with his own group. Darby was also responsible for writing the four songs Elvis sang in *Love Me Tender*, although he credited them to his wife Vera Matson and to Elvis, who took his customary co-writing credit.

Elvis with the Jordanaires. L-R Gordon Stoker, Hoyt Hawkins, Neal Mathews, Hugh Jarrett. 1956.

'Love Me Tender' itself was based on an 1861 civil war ballad, 'Aura Lee', and on 3 November 1956, it effortlessly replaced 'Hound Dog' as America's new No.1 record. This was something of an historic event – it was one of only three times in nearly half a century of *Billboard* charts that an artist has managed to succeed themselves at No.1. The Beatles did it in 1964, and Boyz II Men in 1992, but, as with so many landmark events in the history of rock'n'roll, Elvis did it first.

As the first Elvis ballad to become a hit, 'Love Me Tender' momentarily papered over the image of the sexy hip-swivelling singer and the threatening rock'n'roller out to undermine the American way of life. The song emphasised, perhaps for the first time, the full richness of Elvis Presley's singing voice. This was Elvis relaxed and in control, here was Elvis crooning – it's no coincidence that 'Love Me Tender' was the song Frank Sinatra chose to sing on the 1960 TV special to welcome Elvis out of the Army.

The poignancy of 'Love Me Tender' was heightened further by the death of Elvis' character in

The Colonel, back left, checks the figures as the guys from the movie company get an autograph from Captain Elvis.

the film – although he was resurrected, in classic Hollywood style, as a spectral figure crooning the title song over the end credits. Although set in 1865, *Love Me Tender* also featured a couple of up-tempo rockabilly-style numbers, 'We're Gonna Move' and 'Let Me', but it was the title song that Elvis fans took to their hearts.

As a first-time actor, Elvis made a decent fist of his role as Clint Reno, and it is intriguing to speculate just where he might have gone if he had been allowed the same creative control over his film roles as he had over his musical direction at the time.

Spencer Tracy and Marlon Brando were among his own favourite actors, but towering above all the rest was the memory of the late James Dean – 'a genius' in Elvis' estimation. Dean's death in a car crash in September 1955, at the age of only 24, had sent Hollywood into spasm: not since the death of Rudolph Valentino 30 years before had such scenes of uncontrolled fan hysteria been witnessed. The public reaction was all the more extraordinary because only one film starring James Dean had been released prior to his untimely death – although *East Of Eden* was followed in 1956 by *Rebel Without A Cause* and *Giant*, a trio that cemented James Dean as the iconoclastic screen idol of the decade.

'HE WAS AN INTEGRATOR. ELVIS WAS A BLESSING. THEY WOULDN'T LET BLACK MUSIC THROUGH. HE OPENED THE DOOR FOR BLACK MUSIC'

Little Richard

Such was the gap left by Dean that at one time the Robert Altman documentary *The James Dean Story* was to feature a young actor playing Dean, and the actor studio chiefs wanted for the role was Elvis Presley. In the end, however, Altman brought Dean himself back to life by utilising existing footage.

Elvis remained spellbound by the James Dean legend – on arriving in Hollywood, he was spotted kneeling before *Rebel Without A Cause* director Nick Ray, spouting whole chunks of the script he had

The first album sleeve – much admired and much copied.

learned by heart. And once he started off on his own movie career, he set out to cultivate Dean's friends – among his earliest Hollywood acquaintances were Nick Adams, one of the many actors groomed as a possible successor to Dean, and Natalie Wood, who had starred alongside Dean in *Rebel Without A Cause.*

In the early days, Elvis was surprisingly serious in his approach to film acting. On *Love Me Tender* he eagerly picked up on-camera techniques from co-stars Richard Egan and Mildred Dunnock – but he knew that the critics were just waiting for him to falter in his new career.

To make matters worse, the cinematic competition in 1956 was strong: Don Siegel's timeless *Invasion Of The Body Snatchers*; John Ford's classic western *The Searchers*; the epic *War & Peace*; the star-studded *Around The World In 80 Days* and the controversial *And God Created Woman* (starring ingénue Brigitte Bardot) were a few of the other titles on release. But, in the end, it was Elvis who had the last laugh.

Nearly 600 prints of *Love Me Tender* were shipped out; the film recovered its production costs within four days; and in a few short months it proved itself the second most successful film of 1956, beaten only by Elvis' hero, the late James Dean, in *Giant.*

There was no denying that Elvis was now seriously big business. By the end of 1956, in addition to one of the year's most successful movies, Elvis Presley had been responsible for ten Top 20 singles – including 26 weeks spent at No.1. He had sold more than twelve million singles and nearly three million albums in America alone.

The A–Z of Elvis

D is for Driving

The three things that Elvis liked to do most of all were eat, shoot his guns and drive. The first and last of these activities were closely associated with his beloved mother Gladys. When she died, age 46, she was blimp-shaped and sized. Food, so often in short supply during Elvis' deprived childhood, became a huge comfort for the ailing Gladys, who could probably barely believe her luck at the ready supply. The act of eating his favourite deep-fried banana and peanut butter sandwiches provided a direct and deeply buried link to his long-lost mother for Elvis. It seems that driving his car might have, too. According to Gladys both she and Elvis learned to drive at the same time, in the same car; he was nine at the time. Vernon was 'working in Memphis', they needed to know how to get around without him, so mother and son would drive a mile each along dirt tracks, taking turns at the wheel. Unsurprisingly, after those hot, intimate afternoons behind the wheel with his beloved mom, Elvis passed his driving test age sixteen at the first attempt in his uncle's car. Although his first job was working in a munitions factory, after a few weeks he took a pay cut of almost half to drive a truck delivering electronic goods for Crown Electrical. Elvis' first car, a second-hand white-over-pink Cadillac was bought on HP after 'That's Alright (Mama)' had become a local hit. It lasted a few weeks before the handbrake stuck, caught fire and ignited the rear end of the car while Elvis was driving. The petrol tank blew up. The replacement car was a pink Cadillac bought ostensibly for his mother, but driven, like all the cars he bought for Gladys, by himself. As he grew richer he would buy any and every car that took his fancy, letting other people in his entourage actually do the haggling and transactions, often buying two or more of the same model in order to give them to friends, lovers and members of his entourage. Most of Elvis' cars were American but there was also a Mercedes limousine, a Rolls-Royce and a Ferrari Dino. When awake and bored, often in the middle of the night, Elvis liked nothing better than taking a car full of friends for a drive around Memphis, stopping for burgers on the way home. He also liked to ride his various Harley Davidson motorcycles around Memphis with a pack of minders in tow. The last fan photograph taken of the King is of him driving Lisa Marie back into Graceland at around 6.30 a.m., eight days before he died. They were returning from a trip to the Libertyland fairground, which he'd hired for a private party. The last car Elvis owned was a 1977 Cadillac Seville, in two-tone burgundy and silver with white leather interior.

TOO MUCH

Written by Lee Rosenberg, Bernard Weinman

Recorded 2 September 1956 at Radio Recorders Studios, Hollywood

Guitar: Scotty Moore, Elvis Presley
Bass: Bill Black
Drums: D.J. Fontana
Piano: Gordon Stoker
Vocals: The Jordanaires

Released 4 January 1957

RCA had now accepted that their rock'n'roll sensation was more than just a flash in the pan, and with every single track from Elvis' first LP already released either as a single or an EP, they were pleading for new product.

Unhappy with the facilities available on the 20th Century Fox soundstage, Elvis decided to block-book an independent studio in Hollywood for a three-day session in September 1956. As usual, he began by warming up with a selection of gospel favourites he recalled from shows at the Ellis Auditorium in Memphis. He would then run through whichever of the current crop of pop hits had taken his fancy – songs by Gene Vincent, Jackie Wilson and Carl Perkins. Finally, RCA's Steve Sholes would present the singer with a selection of newly written songs culled from the Hill & Range song catalogue, in which Elvis had a share.

Throughout the formative years of his career, Elvis was scrupulous in his choice of material and painstaking in its recording. Even though the pressures on him were mounting day by day – with a constant clamour of demands from film studios, record labels and his increasingly high public profile – he was determined that every record release would match up to the high standards that he had always set himself.

The three days spent at Radio Recorders studios in Hollywood in September 1956 were productive – as well as the No.1 single 'Too Much', Elvis also recorded the material for his second LP, simply titled *Elvis,* which was released the following month and went on to sell an unprecedented half-million copies within days of its release. Among the songs cut were a version of the Red Foley tear-jerker 'Old Shep' – the first song Elvis had ever sung in public, aged ten at the 1945 Mississippi-Alabama State Fair.

It took a dozen takes before 'Too Much' sounded right to Elvis' ears, but the final version went on to

Too Much

The King in front of his palace: Elvis at Graceland.

give him his first No.1 of 1957. In under a year, Elvis had conquered the charts (pop, R&B and country), television, and cinema; he seemed truly unstoppable.

'Too Much' may not have carried the knock-out punch of 'Heartbreak Hotel' or 'Hound Dog', but it still breathes firc and fervour. Elvis is sultry and clearly in control, and there's an uncharacteristically frenzied solo from Scotty Moore – no wonder his later solo album was called *The Guitar That Changed The World!* 'Too Much' continued the momentum that had transformed Elvis Presley from an enthusiastic teenage crooner into the most talked-about entertainment phenomenon in showbiz history.

'WHEN HE STARTED, HE COULDN'T SPELL TENNESSEE. NOW HE OWNS IT'

Bob Hope

Released at last, The Million Dollar Quartet recordings L-R: Jerry Lee Lewis, Carl Perkins, Elvis and Johnny Cash.

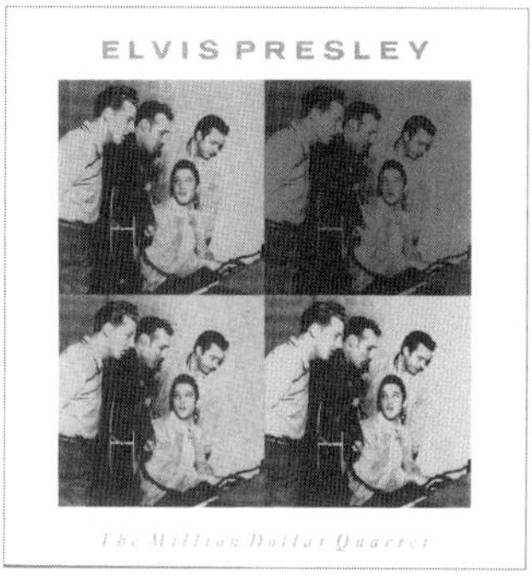

A month before the release of 'Too Much', Elvis was on holiday back home in Memphis and on a whim dropped in at his old stomping ground, Sam Phillips' Sun Studios. Elvis was keen to talk up his new single, and remind Sam that the B-side of 'Too Much', 'Playing For Keeps', was a song on which Sam would enjoy publishing royalties.

Carl Perkins was also in that day, recording some new songs for Sun, and the piano player on the session was a blond boy from Louisiana who was just about to release his first single on Sun – Jerry Lee Lewis. When Elvis dropped in and fellow Sun artiste Johnny Cash was photographed taking an interest in the proceedings, the legend of the Million Dollar Quartet was born – although in truth, Cash was nowhere to be heard on the session, the Man In Black having popped out to do some Christmas shopping.

Elvis had returned to Sun as the reigning king of rock'n'roll. But while they ran through current songs by Chuck Berry and Fats Domino, most of the songs the quartet worked out on at that historic session were soaked in gospel roots – songs like 'Old Rugged Cross', 'I Won't Have To Cross Jordan Alone' and 'Down By The Riverside'. Elvis, incidentally, was seated at the piano until forced to relinquish his place to the cocky Jerry Lee.

A newspaper reporter from the *Memphis Press Scimitar* observed the impromptu jam session and came up with the name The Million Dollar Quartet, but by the time his piece appeared the following day, the event was already history and the quartet never played together again. Over the years, the session has become the stuff of myth. Like Bob Dylan's *Basement Tapes*, The Beach Boys' *Smile* and The Beatles' *Get Back* sessions, The Million Dollar Quartet became one of the few genuine lost treasures of rock'n'roll.

The release of the music created that day was held up by the question of just who controlled the copyright and, of course, the mystery only served to heighten the session's legendary status. As The Million Dollar Quartet only ever convened at Sun Studios, it was assumed that Sam Phillips had the final say. When Sam sold Sun in 1969 a release was anticipated, but once again, legal problems loomed. It wasn't until 1981 that some of the recordings finally surfaced on a UK label. Of course, when fans finally got to hear the album, they discovered that it hardly merited its legend – although despite this the entire session has been remastered and made available on CD.

The Million Dollar Quartet session broke up in the late afternoon, and Elvis went off to spend Christmas at the Memphis home he had purchased for himself and his parents at 1034 Audubon Drive. The only material from that afternoon ever to appear on an official Elvis Presley release was his take on Lowell Fulsom's 'Reconsider Baby', which was included on 1992's *The Complete 50s Masters.*

Soon after 'Too Much' reached No.1 in America, Elvis returned to Hollywood to begin his next film. Before leaving Memphis he found time to buy another property: Graceland, the mansion that would be his home for the rest of his life.

In barely two years, Elvis had gone from his parents' $50-a-month apartment to a Memphis mansion. Little more than a hundred weeks had passed between driving a truck for the Crown Electric Company in Memphis and being the most famous face in America.

The A–Z of Elvis

E is for Elvisly Yours

The brainchild of Sid Shaw – a former street trader, albeit one with a degree in economics from Essex University – Elvisly Yours struck a blow for the right to produce non-Elvis Presley Enterprise Inc-endorsed products in 1999 when it won a landmark victory in the British High Court of Appeal. In 1979 Sid registered Elvisly Yours as a trademark for selling Elvis posters in local markets before extending the trademark to cover all manner of other merchandising. The main reason that EPE lost their case against Sid was that he got there first with the trademarks on the goods and they didn't have his history in selling Elvis trinkets (they registered their trademark in the UK in 1983). The judge decided that people buy Elvis memorabilia because it has Elvis' face on it, not because EPE endorse it, and decided that freedom to trade should rule. The major point that the court made was that 'There is no general right to character exploitation enjoyed exclusively by the celebrity in the UK. There should be no a priori assumption that only a celebrity or his successors may ever market (or license) his own characters. Monopolies should not be so readily created.' Elvisly Yours continues to thrive and in 2000 they extended a license to a credit card manufactured and run by the Bank of Scotland.

ALL SHOOK UP

Written by Otis Blackwell, Elvis Presley

Recorded 12 January 1957 at Radio Recorders Studios, Hollywood

Guitar: Scotty Moore, Elvis Presley
Bass: Bill Black
Drums: D.J. Fontana
Piano: Gordon Stoker
Vocals: The Jordanaires

Released 22 March 1957

By this stage in his career, chances were that if Elvis had released an album of himself reading from the Memphis & District telephone directory it would have gone gold. But despite the demands of his hectic filming schedule, which had now replaced the grinding monotony of touring, Elvis still found time to exercise rigorous quality control over the music RCA kept on demanding from him.

Everyone over twenty was still a bit wary of 'the kid with the sideburns', but even the hard-bitten studio engineers were impressed by the commitment Elvis brought to recording sessions. Despite the pressure on him to churn out large quantities of new material, the boy displayed an obvious dedication to maintaining the quality of his output, eagerly and patiently pursuing just the *right* sound – the sound he could hear so clearly in his own head.

Returning to Hollywood in January 1957 to begin filming his second feature, *Loving You,* Elvis managed to slot in two days of recording. It was his first time in the recording studio for four months, but the music that emerged once again displayed the sheer versatility of Elvis' voice: on the one hand, the raucous rock'n'roll of 'All Shook Up', the sprightly 'Got A Lot O' Livin' To Do', and the downright dirty 'Mean Woman Blues'; and on the other, *Peace In The Valley,* an EP of inspirational music that also emerged from these sessions.

'All Shook Up', which would give Elvis a No.1 hit on both sides of the Atlantic, is probably the record for which those sessions are best remembered today. Legend has it that writer Otis Blackwell originally came up with the idea for the song after someone in the publisher's office fizzed up a bottle of cola and challenged him to write a song about it. Ironically, although Blackwell went on to write some of Elvis' best-known material – several of which featured Elvis as co-author – the two men never met.

All Shook Up

The King in black. Elvis shows off his moves with the microphone stand as the girls scream.

By 1957 Elvis was so famous that he had to hire the Memphis Libertyland Fairgrounds at night for his and friends' amusement.

Blackwell died in May 2002, as this book was being written, but he will always be remembered for creating the song that cemented Elvis Presley's reputation as a superstar, giving him his first UK No.1 and remaining at the top of the American charts for an unbroken run of eight weeks – the longest stretch for which any Elvis single would hold the No.1 slot. In total, 'All Shook Up' remained on *Billboard*'s charts for 30 weeks, enabling it to claim yet another record: the longest chart run of any Elvis single.

British record-buyers were, however, proving more reluctant to embrace rock'n'roll. For most teenagers, their only access to the new music was through the pages of *Melody Maker*, the musicians' bible that sold 110,000 copies every week – and early on, *Melody Maker* had shown itself to have a real downer on the rockers. The paper's review of an earlier Elvis single gives a flavour: 'when 'Hound Dog' was released – and believe me, "released" is the word – I sat up and took rather special notice. Lo, these many times have I heard bad records, but for sheer repulsiveness,

'ON STAGE HE ENCOMPASSED EVERYTHING – HE WAS LAUGHING AT THE WORLD AND HE WAS LAUGHING AT HIMSELF, BUT AT THE SAME TIME HE WAS DEAD SERIOUS'

Bruce Springsteen

coupled with the monotony of incoherence, "Hound Dog" hit a new low in my experience!'

The success of 'All Shook Up' proved that Elvis was beginning to reach out to British record-buyers by early 1957 – if not to the jazz-loving journalists. But even the *Melody Maker* readers' poll that year voted Frank Sinatra International Best Male Vocalist, while Elvis Presley was left languishing at No.14.

'All Shook Up' finally reached No.1 on the British chart in July 1957, deposing skiffle king Lonnie Donegan. Incidentally, Elvis' B-side, 'That's When Your Heartaches Begin', cut at the same session as 'All Shook Up', was a full version of the Ink Spots song he had recorded on a $3.98 acetate at Sun Studios barely three years before.

The release of 'All Shook Up' was something of a turning point in Presley's early career, marking the moment when Elvis finally left behind the three-piece rockabilly sound he had developed at Sun, and that he had carried over onto his early RCA records. From now on, much of the Elvis Presley sound would be characterised instead by the lush vocal backing of The Jordanaires.

With its infectious 'uh-hu-huh' vocal fills, irresistible swaying melody and Elvis' stylishly nervy lead, 'All Shook Up' remains one of the great Elvis singles. Hearing it, you can't help but picture the young Elvis, his dark sideburns framing that famous, still beautiful face on which a smile plays, twitching in time to the music. Otis Blackwell's song went on to be recorded by Ry Cooder, Suzi Quatro and Jeff Beck among others, but the definitive version will always remain that of Elvis Presley.

The A–Z of Elvis

F is for Flying Elvi

A ten-man skydiving team first seen in the film *Honeymoon In Vegas* (1992) starring Nicolas Cage, James Caan and Sarah Jessica Parker, the experienced skydivers fall to earth dressed as Vegas-era Elvis in white, spangly jumpsuits with silver sun-specs and jet-black wigs. Although invented for the film by writer/director Andy Bergman, the Flying Elvi now earn hundreds of thousands of dollars a year promoting the launch of new products and openings of various malls and casinos in the US. They have jumped from 10,000 feet up to publicise, among other merchandise, the launch of a new Elvis Presley slot machine, the Visa Las Vegas credit card, and the Barbie loves Elvis collectors doll set.

(LET ME BE YOUR) TEDDY BEAR

Written by Kal Mann, Bernie Lowe

Recorded 24 January 1957 at Radio Recorders Studios, Hollywood

Guitar: Scotty Moore, Elvis Presley
Bass: Bill Black
Drums: D.J. Fontana
Piano: Dudley Brooks
Vocals: The Jordanaires

Released 11 June 1957

Teddy Bear

Elvis' Midas touch had not deserted him, and the success of his first film, *Love Me Tender,* meant that within two months of its release Elvis was back in Hollywood shooting a second movie.

This one had started out with the title *Lonesome Cowboy*; later became *Running Wild*; and was changed again when producer Hal Wallis heard the Leiber and Stoller ballad that became the film's theme song and remembered the extraordinary response 'Love Me Tender' had provoked. So finally the title was decided, and *Loving You* it was.

The plot – 'Deke Rivers is a small-town boy who unexpectedly sings his way into fame' – didn't tax Elvis unduly, but the storyline soon became the template for pretty much every other rock'n'roll movie of the decade. In fairness, *Loving You* was not nearly as bad as it sounds, displaying an exuberance and vivacity that Elvis rarely captured on film again, and containing some of Elvis' best-ever film songs – like 'Got A Lot O' Livin' To Do', 'Party' and 'Mean Woman Blues'. The Deke Rivers performance scenes even managed to convey a faint echo of the frenzied energy of the young Elvis on stage.

In 1942 Hal Wallis had produced the immortal *Casablanca* and, as a result, Bogart and Bergman would always have Paris. Sadly, Elvis was never that lucky. Although Wallis always made sure that his new star was surrounded by Hollywood stalwarts (in the case of *Loving You,* Wendell Corey, who had recently appeared in Hitchcock's *Rear Window,* and the sultry Lizabeth Scott) Elvis later came to resent the fact that Wallis' quality productions (such as *Becket* starring Richard Burton and Peter O'Toole) were subsidised by his own work on simplistic vehicles like *Loving You.*

The hours spent watching his heroes – Marlon Brando, James Dean, Montgomery Clift – on screen,

Elvis performing for radio, 1956.

A French picture sleeve single release of 'Loving You' c/w '(Let Me Be Your) Teddy Bear', 1980s.

had taught Elvis that much of their cool charisma came from a refusal to smile for the camera. 'I don't know anything about Hollywood,' Elvis admitted at the time, 'but I know you can't be sexy if you smile. You can't be a rebel if you grin!' So Elvis buttoned down his lip.

The dedication and focus Elvis brought to his role ensured that *Loving You* remains one of his strongest films, as well as one of his personal favourites. And as a thank-you to his parents who were visiting him in Hollywood at the time, he gave them a tiny cameo appearance in the film – you can see them, clearly in shot, clapping along during the film's final concert. Sadly though, Elvis was so devastated by his mother's death the following year that he couldn't bring himself to watch *Loving You* ever again.

'HE HAD SO MUCH ENERGY WE HAD TO SIT UP NIGHTS TO WEAR HIM OUT SO WE COULD SLEEP' **Scotty Moore, guitarist**

Somehow a rumour started to circulate suggesting that, although he was now aged 22, widely recognised as the sexiest man on the planet, and at the centre of a worldwide rock'n'roll phenomenon, Elvis Presley still collected teddy bears. Thousands of bears began to arrive in every post, along with a song from two Philadelphia writers. The bears were packed off to the National Foundation for Infantile Paralysis, but the song stayed.

Besides his two-month filming schedule, Elvis had recording commitments in Hollywood at the beginning of 1957. The bulk of the *Loving You* soundtrack had already been cut, but one lengthy session produced a typical mixture of material, including a classic rock'n'roll cover (Fats Domino's 'Blueberry Hill') and a heartfelt gospel interpretation ('It Is No Secret What God Can Do'). And then, of course, there was the bright and breezy 'Teddy Bear'. The song came courtesy of Bernie Lowe and his partner Kal Mann, who besides being a songwriter enjoyed a parallel career as head of the Cameo/Parkway label. Together the pair went on to write such hits as Charlie Grace's 'Butterfly', Chubby Checker's 'Let's Twist Again' and The Dovells' 'Bristol Stomp'.

'Teddy Bear' was designed to satisfy Elvis' legions of younger fans, those who were still sending him teddy bears of all conceivable kinds by the sackload. The lyrics deliberately cast Elvis in a rather different light: pliable and easily led rather than jungle-tough. Certainly, heard alongside the snarling, sensual 'Mean Woman Blues' on the *Loving You* soundtrack LP, 'Teddy Bear' comes across as marshmallow-soft – but that was always the intention. Elvis has fun with the song, The Jordanaires supply the fills flawlessly, and jazz veteran Dudley Brooks' piano swings the song along. At the end of the day '(Let Me Be Your) Teddy Bear' barely exceeded 100 seconds; yet within three weeks of its release, it had sold a million copies in America alone.

If anyone still needed convincing, the double-whammy of *Loving You* and 'Teddy Bear' proved beyond doubt that Elvis Presley was no passing craze.

The A–Z of Elvis

G is for Guns

Like many a Southern good ol' boy before him, and many after, Elvis had a thing for guns. As a kid he'd wanted a .22. In the Army he got to be a tank gunner. At Graceland he built a shooting gallery in the back garden and would often take a few of his 40-plus weapons out for a few rounds, regardless of what time it was, day or night. While on tour Elvis would shoot out lights and televisions for fun. He'd even threaten his closest friends and minders with one of his guns, such as the Army-issue .45 that he kept on him at all times, or the Smith & Wesson .38 that had TCB and a lightning bolt engraved on the handle (Taking Care of Business in a flash). Because of his fear of kidnap or assassination, Elvis liked to be prepared. He kept M-16s, handguns, rifles and even a sub-machine gun at home. According to his step-brother David Stanley, after his appointment as a narcotics agent by President Nixon in 1970 Elvis set up silhouette targets in the back garden of Graceland (next to the house fuel tank) and spent the day blasting at them with everything he had in his gun cupboard. He was wearing a cape and wrap-around sunglasses at the time.

JAILHOUSE ROCK

Written by Jerry Leiber and Mike Stoller

Recorded 30 April 1957 at Radio Recorders Studios, Hollywood

Guitar: Scotty Moore, Elvis Presley
Bass: Bill Black
Drums: D.J. Fontana
Piano: Dudley Brooks
Vocals: The Jordanaires

Released 24 September 1957

Jailhouse Rock

After the sweetness of 'Teddy Bear', came the sharp antidote of *Jailhouse Rock*. Elvis' third film, envisaged as the flip-side of *Loving You*, was shot in stark black and white as opposed to the previous film's lurid colour. And Elvis' character – Vince Everett – though also a singer, was this time surly and self-centred in contrast to the shy and modest character of Deke Rivers.

In true Hollywood fashion, *Jailhouse Rock* had been conceived to cash in on the wider concerns of the American public. Juvenile delinquency was now a term on everybody's lips and juvenile delinquents were associated with rock'n'roll, so it followed that the best place for the world's most famous rock'n'roller was behind bars. As with all Elvis' film work during the 50s, *Jailhouse Rock* suggested that he really did stand a chance as an actor: his surliness was marketable, his sensuality unmistakable, but he was also capable of turning those doe eyes on to an audience and melting their hearts.

It was quite a gamble to make the lead character in *Jailhouse Rock* so rebellious and truculent, and perhaps to emphasise the point that this was not the *real* Elvis, but only Elvis acting, the film was advertised as 'Elvis Presley in his first dramatic singing role'. The pre-publicity promised 'Singing! Fighting! Dancing! Romancing!' – and as if all that weren't enough, the film also gave fans the opportunity to see their idol stripped half-naked and flogged in punishment.

Shooting the movie in black and white was quite a risk too. This was, after all, at a time when the cinema industry was reeling from the first impact of audiences staying at home to watch their television sets – and Hollywood's response had been to fill the enormous cinema screens with larger-than-life Technicolor spectacles.

While *Jailhouse Rock* has more than its fair share of movie clichés, it does also have some redeeming scenes and dialogue – fans still relish Elvis' exchange with love interest Judy Tyler, when she snaps: 'How dare you think such cheap tactics would work with me!' only to have Elvis reply: 'That ain't tactics, honey – it's just the beast in me!'

It was indicative of his status that when Elvis moved on to the MGM lot in 1957 to begin filming *Jailhouse Rock*, he was given Clark Gable's old dressing room. Once settled in, it became apparent there was little sympatico between Elvis and Richard Thorpe, the film's veteran director, whose previous work had veered between *The Great Caruso* and *Ivanhoe*. But despite their differences, he steered Elvis safely home, and *Jailhouse Rock* remains high on the list of Elvis fans' favourites.

Three films on, Elvis was genuinely keen to pursue screen acting as a career – and he was much flattered when Robert Mitchum sought him out to play the role of his son in the bootlegging drama *Thunder Road*. There was also talk of Elvis starring alongside Sidney Poitier in the drama *The Defiant Ones* – but the Colonel declined that one on the grounds that there were no songs. There was even the enticing prospect of Elia Kazan directing Elvis in a film musical specially written for him by Leiber and Stoller, but that got nixed too. For a career blessed with so many record-breaking moments, there were an enormous number of missed opportunities.

An original UK single of 'Jailhouse Rock' with distinctive triangular middle piece.

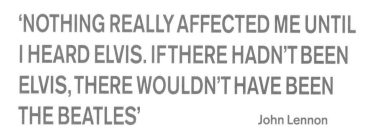

'NOTHING REALLY AFFECTED ME UNTIL I HEARD ELVIS. IF THERE HADN'T BEEN ELVIS, THERE WOULDN'T HAVE BEEN THE BEATLES'

John Lennon

'ELVIS HAD THE POWER OVER PEOPLE'S IMAGINATIONS THAT WOULD ENABLE HIM TO OBTAIN HIGH OFFICE'

Richard Nixon

Jailhouse Rock

Jerry Leiber and Mike Stoller already had a rock-solid reputation as songwriters by the time their path crossed that of Elvis Presley. The two writers, just a couple of years older than Elvis himself, appreciated the King covering a couple of their songs on *Loving You*, but the appreciation was almost purely financial. Steeped in a love of black culture, the pair had been unimpressed by Elvis' version of 'Hound Dog' and aesthetically they considered the Memphis Flash to be merely a flash in the pan.

It was no surprise, then, that when Leiber and Stoller were asked to come up with material for Elvis' next film, they procrastinated more than a little. 'In the spring of 1957,' Jerry Leiber remembered, 'we were summoned to New York in order to discuss and write the score for a new Presley film. We had been in New York for about a week but had not settled down to write anything for the new film, New York was just too exciting. We were about to leave the hotel room for another assault on Manhattan, when Jean Aberbach of Presley Music barged in. He pushed a large sofa in front of the door, blocking the entrance, and with that informed us that we were not leaving the room until we had finished the score and placed it in his hands. Mike and I shrugged and went to the rented upright piano in the corner of the room and while Jean pretended to doze on the couch, we hammered out 'Jailhouse Rock', 'Treat Me Nice', 'I Want To Be Free' and 'Baby I Don't Care'!'

The ambiguous lyrics of the title song, particularly the line about one inmate telling another that 'you're the cutest little jailbird I ever did see' were a deliberate piece of Lieber and Stoller mischief. As Stoller laster remarked, 'Ambiguity is a big part of Jerry's work.' It was Leiber and Stoller's revenge on Elvis for his version of Hound Dog.

When the songwriters finally got to meet Elvis, though – at Radio Recorders Studios in Hollywood – it was a very different matter. Leiber and Stoller were struck by the young singer's knowledge of and fondness for the blues music they themselves loved so much; Stoller even ended up appearing in the finished film, playing the part of Elvis' piano player.

A typical Elvis publicity still of the late 50s.

In 1980 on the sleeve of *Elvis Presley Sings Leiber & Stoller*, Mike Stoller recalled that first meeting: 'At first we just talked generally about music and making records, then we drifted over to the piano and got to know each other better. Elvis and I played some four-handed blues piano for a while ... Jerry Leiber kicked off a run-through of 'Jailhouse Rock'. It was starting to feel good. Jerry made some suggestions ... and we tried it again. It was great. Elvis said, "OK, let's make it." Jerry ran into the control booth and set the tempo, snapping his fingers over the intercom.' The pair were particularly impressed with Elvis' tenacity in the recording studio: 'Jailhouse Rock' he got in just six takes, but '(You're So Square) Baby I Don't Care' took no less than 22 attempts before the singer was completely satisfied.

Right from the start, before Elvis even sings a note, 'Jailhouse Rock' is up there, kicking off with one of the most recognisable openings in rock'n'roll. D.J. Fontana's drums crash like cell doors slamming shut ('I tried to think of someone on a chain-gang smashing rocks' the drummer later recalled); Scotty Moore solos furiously; and Elvis is magnificent.

The version of 'Jailhouse Rock' heard in the film was discordantly different from the familiar chart-topping single. You can hear the film version on the 1997 CD re-release of the soundtrack, but despite the jarring brass and vocal insertions, it lacks the impact of the more-familiar stripped-down version. Nevertheless, the scene with Elvis and his fellow inmates singing 'Jailhouse Rock' is one of the key scenes in rock'n'roll cinema and the song owes much of its continued success to the film in which it first appeared.

L-R: Vernon Presley, Elvis aged around 9 years, Gladys Presley.

Legend has it that Elvis choreographed that sequence himself. In fact, choreographer Alex Romero had already mapped out some moves in the style of Gene Kelly or Fred Astaire, which he demonstrated to Elvis, only to be met with a polite, but emphatic 'No!' So Romero played some of Elvis' hits and asked the singer to demonstrate just how he moved on stage. He watched carefully as Elvis mimed, made detailed notes, and came back the next morning having prepared a sequence that would enshrine Elvis Presley's image on the cinema screen for all time. The only problem came when Elvis got so carried away filming the routine that he swallowed a tooth cap and had to be taken to hospital to have it removed.

Besides the unforgettable title track, *Jailhouse Rock* also featured a couple of other Leiber and Stoller classics. One in particular, '(You're So Square) Baby I Don't Care', went on to have a life of its own – it was covered by everyone from Buddy Holly to Iggy Pop – although Elvis himself always preferred the B-side of 'Jailhouse Rock', 'Treat Me Nice'.

In Britain too, 'Jailhouse Rock' carved itself a little slice of chart history, when in January 1958 it became the first single ever to enter the UK charts straight at No.1. With advance orders running at an unprecedented 250,000, the pressing plants were already struggling to meet the demand – and in the event, 'Jailhouse Rock' went on to sell over half a million copies during the first week of its release alone.

Jailhouse Rock owed much of its success to the songs of Leiber and Stoller, and from that moment on, their names became so closely linked with that of Elvis that RCA decided to release the *Elvis Presley Sings Leiber & Stoller* album. The cover shot was a given: taken on the MGM lot in 1957, it has Elvis studying the sheet music of 'Jailhouse Rock' flanked by the song's authors. It was only after a great deal of delicate negotiation that the cover went ahead and, allegedly, it remains to this day the only Elvis Presley album to show anyone apart from Elvis on its cover.

The A–Z of Elvis

H is for Hawaii

Apart from his time spent in Germany in 1960 while serving in the Army, Elvis only ever travelled within the confines of America. There was one brief tour of Canada in 1957, but that was it. The same year he also played his first gigs on what was once foreign soil, however, and fell in love with the only exotic destination he ever knew: Hawaii. He made four movies there – *Blue Hawaii* in 1961, *Girls! Girls! Girls!* a year later, *Paradise Hawaiian Style* in 1965 and *Aloha From Hawaii,* the concert film broadcast across the world in 1973. He bought property on Oahu Island and outside Honolulu, where he spent his honeymoon rolling around the surf with Priscilla. The Islands played a big part in re-establishing Elvis as the foremost performer in America when he came out of the Army in 1960. After performing in Memphis for charity, Elvis and the Colonel decided that a Pearl Harbor Memorial concert at the Bloch Arena, Pearl Harbor would be the next live appearance. All ticket proceeds went towards a memorial for the men killed on board the USS Arizona. The posters for the show depicted Elvis in his now famous gold lamé suit, although for the concert he wore only the jacket with black dress pants. The gig was the first time that RCA used the 'Aloha, Elvis' tag, too. The two days in January 1973 that were recorded for broadcast as *Aloha from Hawaii* were the last dates Elvis played in the state. For the rest of the 70s he would go around the same circuit on the US mainland, punctuated by month-plus residencies in Las Vegas. But Elvis continued to vacation in Hawaii, and in March of 1977 he took the last holiday of his life in Honolulu.

DON'T

Written by Jerry Leiber and Mike Stoller

Recorded 6 September 1957 at Radio Recorders Studios, Hollywood

Guitar: Scotty Moore, Elvis Presley
Bass: Bill Black
Drums: D.J. Fontana
Piano: Dudley Brooks
Vocals: The Jordanaires

Released 7 January 1958

Having already given Elvis two No.1 hits, with 'Hound Dog' and 'Jailhouse Rock', Leiber and Stoller were the obvious choice for the next Presley single. This time around, impressed by the pair's abilities and hands-on enthusiasm, Elvis asked them to write a pretty ballad for him to record. 'Don't' was the result.

Looking back in 1980, Mike Stoller recalled: 'When they started filming *Jailhouse Rock* I got a call to come out to MGM and play the role of Elvis' piano player. On the set one day, Elvis asked me if Jerry and I would write a long song for him. We wrote "Don't" on the weekend and on Monday when I played it for him, Elvis smiled and said, "That's real pretty, that's just what I wanted."'

Elvis had set aside a couple of days for recording during the filming of *Jailhouse Rock* and it was during one of these sessions that 'Don't' was cut. His record label had been keen for him to record an album of Christmas songs, and to get Elvis in the mood they even supplied a Christmas tree with presents underneath for the September session. It all went swimmingly and, over the two days, Elvis nailed definitive versions of 'Blue Christmas' and 'Santa Claus Is Back In Town' as well as a number of other festive standards. However, so potent was Elvis' image as a rock'n'roll rebel, that Irving Berlin, the composer of 'White Christmas', took issue with the teen idol covering his song and instructed radio stations across America to cease playing it.

Recording an album's worth of cool Yule treats was another example of Elvis' pioneering role – he would be followed by The Beach Boys, Phil Spector, The Jackson 5 and many others who went on to make Christmas albums. The Elvis 'Christmas' sessions of September 1957 also produced 'Treat Me Nice', the B-side of 'Jailhouse Rock'; a sensitive version of Ivory Joe Hunter's 'My Wish Came True'; and 'Don't', Elvis' next No.1 – the first A-side to feature a ballad since 'Love Me Tender', all of a year before.

Elvis on stage with The Jordanaires for the Louisiana Hayride Radio Show, 1956.

'Don't' came quick and easy, in just seven takes. Elvis himself sounds relaxed but, as ever, firmly in control; The Jordanaires supply their trademark wall of voices; and the backing is so laid-back as to sound almost soporific. The image conjured up is one of relaxing before a blazing log fire, while the snow piles up outside the frosted window and the hi-fi softly trickles out Elvis' latest single.

Simple and straightforward as the recording session had been, there was trouble brewing. Long-time sidemen Scotty Moore and Bill Black were feeling unhappy about the way they had been treated since their lives were turned upside down by the explosion of interest in all things Elvis. In the last couple of years they'd played on million-selling records, supported Elvis in concert, and appeared with him on television and film – but they were still being paid little more than the flat fee they had drawn in 1955, when the three of them tore off touring anywhere and everywhere south of the Mason–Dixon line. Elvis' healthy pay cheques now made for very happy reading; unfortunately, those of his hapless musicians didn't.

Although the matter was eventually resolved, relations between them were never quite the same again. But perhaps that was inevitable: so much had happened in such a short space of time, that it was now almost impossible to remember what life had been like just a few years before. As Russian satellites hurtled through space and troops were sent in to desegregate Little Rock, Arkansas, the world itself seemed to be changing before their eyes – but still it seemed as though all America was really interested in was Elvis Presley.

The awkward confrontation with his musicians was only one of a series of problems that Elvis would face over the next few months. In November 1957 he sailed to Hawaii, to play what would prove to be his last concert for four years; *Jailhouse Rock* opened that same month, doing the usual buoyant box-office business; and the following January Elvis once again set off for Hollywood, to begin filming his fourth movie.

King Creole was based on the novel *A Stone For Danny Fisher* by the controversial writer Harold Robbins, and the film's New Orleans locations were intended to lend authenticity to an already gritty narrative. This time, however, shooting couldn't commence until Elvis had deferred his army enlistment – and throughout filming, the threat of the draft hung over his head.

As a healthy young US male, 22-year-old Elvis Presley was clearly eligible for service in the military and rumours had begun seeping out that the most famous young man in America was about to be drafted. The rumours were soon followed by suggestions that Elvis might receive preferential treatment, that his manager would ease him out of the draft; and before long the tone became more critical, accusing the singer of considering himself 'too big' for the Army.

Don't

In the event, Paramount Pictures did manage to gain their boy a 60-day deferment, pointing out to the draft board that considerable sums of money had already been invested in pre-production costs and that without their star, they simply wouldn't have a picture.

Elvis gained two extra months of freedom, but all the while he was nervous about what lay ahead. As to the actual filming, Elvis enjoyed the experience. *King Creole* had the best pedigree of any Elvis Presley film. It was directed by Michael Curtiz, the man responsible for such glorious examples of the Golden Age of Hollywood as *The Adventures of Robin Hood, Yankee Doodle Dandy* and the classic *Casablanca*. The supporting cast included Oscar-nominee Carolyn Jones; Vic Morrow, hot from his triumph in *The Blackboard Jungle;* and Walter Matthau, then already well into his career as one of the movie industry's most respected supporting actors. And the ever-dependable Leiber and Stoller were on hand for the memorable title theme as well as 'Trouble', and the incongruous 'Steadfast, Loyal And True'.

'WHEN I FIRST HEARD ELVIS' VOICE, I JUST KNEW THAT I WASN'T GOING TO WORK FOR ANYBODY; AND NOBODY WAS GOING TO BE MY BOSS'

Bob Dylan

King Creole turned out surprisingly well – and throughout a career in which he made over 30 films, it would remain Elvis' own favourite. But now, with filming complete, there was the matter of his military service to be addressed. Everyone was bidding for Elvis: the Navy offered to form an 'Elvis Presley Company'; the Air Force was willing to let him tour as a recruitment officer. But Elvis stuck with the Army, where he was hoping he might get a chance to enjoy some anonymity – something that had eluded him since the madness took hold two years previously.

'Don't' gave Elvis his last No.1 as a civilian. On 24 March 1958 he reported to the draft board in

Although it looked like a prop at times, Elvis really could play the guitar. Louisiana Hayride Radio Show, 1956.

Memphis and the next day at Fort Chaffee, Arkansas, he was given the drastic GI haircut that removed his trademark sideburns for the duration. Thanks to Colonel Parker, the world's press were there in force to witness the transformation of the world's best-known rock'n'roll idol into Private First Class Presley, E.A., 53310761.

The A–Z of Elvis

I is for I, Lisa Marie

The title of the autobiography of Lisa Marie Presley, a.k.a. Lisa Johansen. Lisa a.k.a. Johansen was, she claims, taken away from Graceland after the death of Elvis and given to a friendly Swedish family to bring up. Her website, http://www.i-lisa-marie.com, states that, 'Trusted family members and friends convinced her it is for her own safety that she must assume a new identity until she comes of an age to take her rightful place as the sole heir of a huge estate.' Which she was ready to do on the publication of her autobiography in 1999. But, of course, she has been 'blocked at every turn by powerful and sinister forces'. As proof that the Lisa Marie Presley that the world recognises – the one who married Michael Jackson, is a scientologist and had well-documented problems with men and drugs etc. – is not the real Lisa Marie, http://www.i-lisa-marie.com lists the 'facts' as follows: 'In 1995 the Swedish newspaper *Aftonbladet* published a report documenting Mrs Jackson's facial proportions in comparison with acknowledged photos of Lisa Marie Presley as a child. The report concludes that Mrs Jackson's forehead is 13% smaller than Lisa Marie Presley's aged nine. In February 1998, the result was confirmed by leading facial identification specialists at the Royal Canadian Mounted Police (RCMP). A new study had been done which established that Mrs Jackson's forehead was 5 to 10 millimetres shorter than Lisa Marie Presley's predicted growth from age nine to adult.' The website also contains photographs of Lisa a.k.a. Johansen that show a certain similarity with Elvis, although none are close up enough to be able to detect plastic surgery scars. Lisa Marie a.k.a. Lisa Johansen states that she has only gone public in order to reconcile herself with her mother and have the 'chance to introduce herself and her children to what is left of the tattered circle of friends and family and the millions of devoted Elvis Presley fans.' You can buy the book on the website at $23 and decide for yourself.

HARD HEADED WOMAN

Written by Claude DeMetrius

Recorded 15 January 1958 at Radio Recorders Studios, Hollywood

Guitar: Scotty Moore
Bass: Bill Black, Neal Matthews
Drums: D.J. Fontana
Trumpet: John Ed Buckner
Trombone: Elmer Schneider
Saxophone: Justin Gordon
Piano: Dudley Brooks
Vocals: The Jordanaires

Released 10 June 1958

Hard Headed Woman

Recorded at the *King Creole* soundtrack sessions, 'Hard Headed Woman' marks one of the last times Elvis really let rip on a film song. A rollicking electric bass fuels his vocal; some snazzy brass punctuates the performance; and lyrically, Elvis takes us from Adam and Eve to Samson and Delilah and along the way bumps into 'that evil Jezebel'. True that it may seem politically incorrect to 21st-century sensibilities, but in 1958 it was taken as read that an independent woman would represent a 'thorn in the side of man!'

In performance, 'Hard Headed Woman' recalled the first song that Elvis had cut at his very first session for RCA – Ray Charles' 'I Got A Woman'. In the brief period since then, he had quickly proved himself adept at handling ballads, R&B covers, hard-hitting rock'n'roll and heartfelt gospel. But on 'Hard Headed Woman' Elvis shed his Hollywood inhibitions and rekindled the old magic that had mesmerised the nation throughout 1956.

With army service beckoning, it seemed like this could be a final farewell to the old Elvis – and 'Hard Headed Woman' marked the end of another era too: it was the last Elvis record ever to be issued as a 78rpm disc. From now on, all Elvis singles would appear on the new-fangled plastic 45s.

By the time 'Hard Headed Woman' reached No.1 in July 1958, Elvis was undergoing basic training at Fort Hood in Texas and despite his successes in the civilian world, the 23-year-old was still uncertain about how he would be received in the military. The sheer incongruity was startling: the world's best-known rock'n'roll star zoomed to No.1 for the tenth time, but far from celebrating, Private Presley was stuck out in the middle of the Texas prairies undertaking carbine practice.

In addition to all his other worries, Elvis was increasingly concerned about his mother's health. As her only surviving son, he was always particularly

Original UK single version of 'Hard Headed Woman'.

close to his mother and on joining the Army had brought his parents with him to live near his base in Texas. Elvis and his father Vernon had learned to cope with the whirlwind that had embraced them, but his mother was nervous and wary of the changes.

Although she was only 46, Gladys Presley had never enjoyed good health: she was overweight, worried constantly about her son, and was already on heavy medication. In Texas, Gladys' health declined and in August she returned to Memphis for treatment. Within days her condition had deteriorated, and in a tragic irony, being America's most famous enlisted man now worked against Elvis. Sick as his mother was, the Army could not be seen to be favouring him by granting him compassionate leave. Had he been just an ordinary soldier, the chances are he would have been rushed home, but as it was he only just managed to get back to Memphis in time to see Gladys before she passed away.

His mother's original illness had been caused by problems with her liver, but in the end it was a heart attack that killed her. Elvis was inconsolable. He wept and wailed for days and was barely able to keep hold

'WHEN ELVIS SANG, HE FELT MORE FULL OF HIMSELF AND MORE COMPLETELY IN TOUCH WITH THE REST OF HUMANITY THAN AT ANY OTHER TIME. ALL OF THIS CAN BE HEARD WITHOUT DELVING TOO DEEPLY INTO ANYTHING ABSTRACT... ELVIS SANG'

Dave Marsh, rock journalist

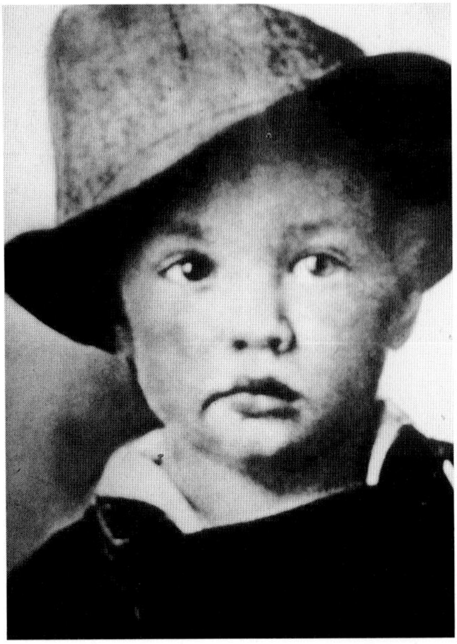

Elvis aged about 3 years, looking like a dustbowl baby.

Hard Headed Woman

of himself. In theory, he had everything he had ever wanted from the world; but now he was just another enlisted man who, in a few short months, had left behind a glamorous film star career and watched his mother die.

Elvis had just about managed to gain control of himself again by October 1958, when the time came for him to depart for overseas service in Germany. Fans had proved themselves able to cope with their idol in the Army, but now with Elvis leaving the country, both he and Colonel Parker were worrying afresh about the long-term effect of his two-year withdrawal from the public eye. No rock'n'roll idol had ever left the stage like that before – if they did disappear, it simply meant they weren't coming back.

RCA's Steve Sholes had been keen to stockpile a batch of new Elvis Presley material, which could then be filtered out gradually during the singer's absence. The canny Colonel Parker went the other way. It was a risky strategy – and one which suggested that the Colonel, at least, believed Elvis had a long career ahead of him. He reasoned that by starving the fans, they'd be all the more hungry for new material when Elvis finally did return.

Eventually a compromise was reached and in June 1958, during a two-week army leave, Elvis flew to Nashville. One all-night session produced a brace of future No.1s – but it was to be his last time in a recording studio for two whole years.

Elvis called-up for the Army; Elvis enlisting in the Army; Elvis' army haircut; Elvis sailing overseas with the Army – all these were big news events. Colonel Parker even issued an *Elvis Sails* EP featuring an edited version of the press conference Elvis had

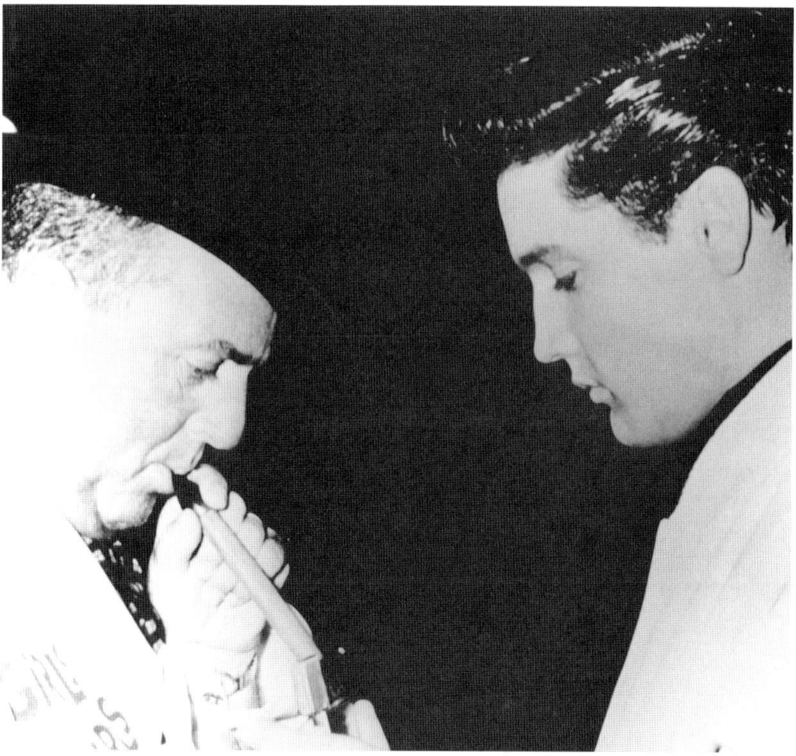

Colonel Tom Parker has his cigar lit by his charge, Elvis.

given prior to his departure for Europe. On television too Elvis' enlistment was a talking point: the popular comedy programme *Sgt Bilko* featured an unmistakable new recruit to the scheming sergeant's company – one 'Elvin Pelvin', who got to sing his big hit, 'Brown Suede Combat Boots'. While in 1960, Broadway welcomed an entire musical show about the enlistment of a rock'n'roll idol into the Army called *Bye Bye Birdie*.

Today, when rock stars spend years fashioning a single album, a two-year hiatus may seem unremarkable. But back in 1958, it was simply unthinkable. What about his popularity while he was in service, Elvis was asked in Memphis just before he was called up – did he think it would slip? 'Well that's the 64 dollar question,' Elvis admitted, 'I wish I knew.'

ONE NIGHT

Written by Dave Bartholomew, Pearl King

Recorded 23 February 1957 at Radio Recorders Studios, Hollywood

Guitar: Scotty Moore, Elvis Presley
Bass: Bill Black
Drums: D.J. Fontana
Piano: Dudley Brooks

Released 21 October 1958

'One Night' was denied the No.1 slot in America on a technicality. Because of the complex system used to compile the US charts, sales were split between it and 'I Got Stung', the record's B-side and one of the tracks Elvis had recorded at his recent session in Nashville. However, there were no such complications to muddy the water across the Atlantic – and in January 1959 'One Night' gave Elvis his third British No.1.

There are over four thousand songs that feature Dave Bartholomew's name on the label. During a songwriting career stretching back over half a century, Bartholomew wrote many of Fats Domino's best-known hits ('Blue Monday', 'Walking To New Orleans'), as well as hits for Ricky Nelson ('I'm Walkin''), Lloyd Price ('Lawdy Miss Clawdy'), and Smiley Lewis ('I Hear You Knockin', later a hit for Dave Edmunds). 'One Night Of Sin' had also been a hit for Smiley Lewis in 1956 and now, with the original lyrics cleaned up a bit, it gave Private Presley another No.1.

In the hard-hitting tradition of 'Hard Headed Woman', 'One Night' was Elvis Presley unleashed, suggesting all manner of libatious thrills for the night ahead. Elvis himself might be safely tucked away in the Army, but any suggestion that his music had been similarly calmed was quickly disproved by 'One Night'. The heavily electrified 12-bar blues benefits from a Presley vocal dripping with lip-smacking delights.

Original UK single 'One Night'.

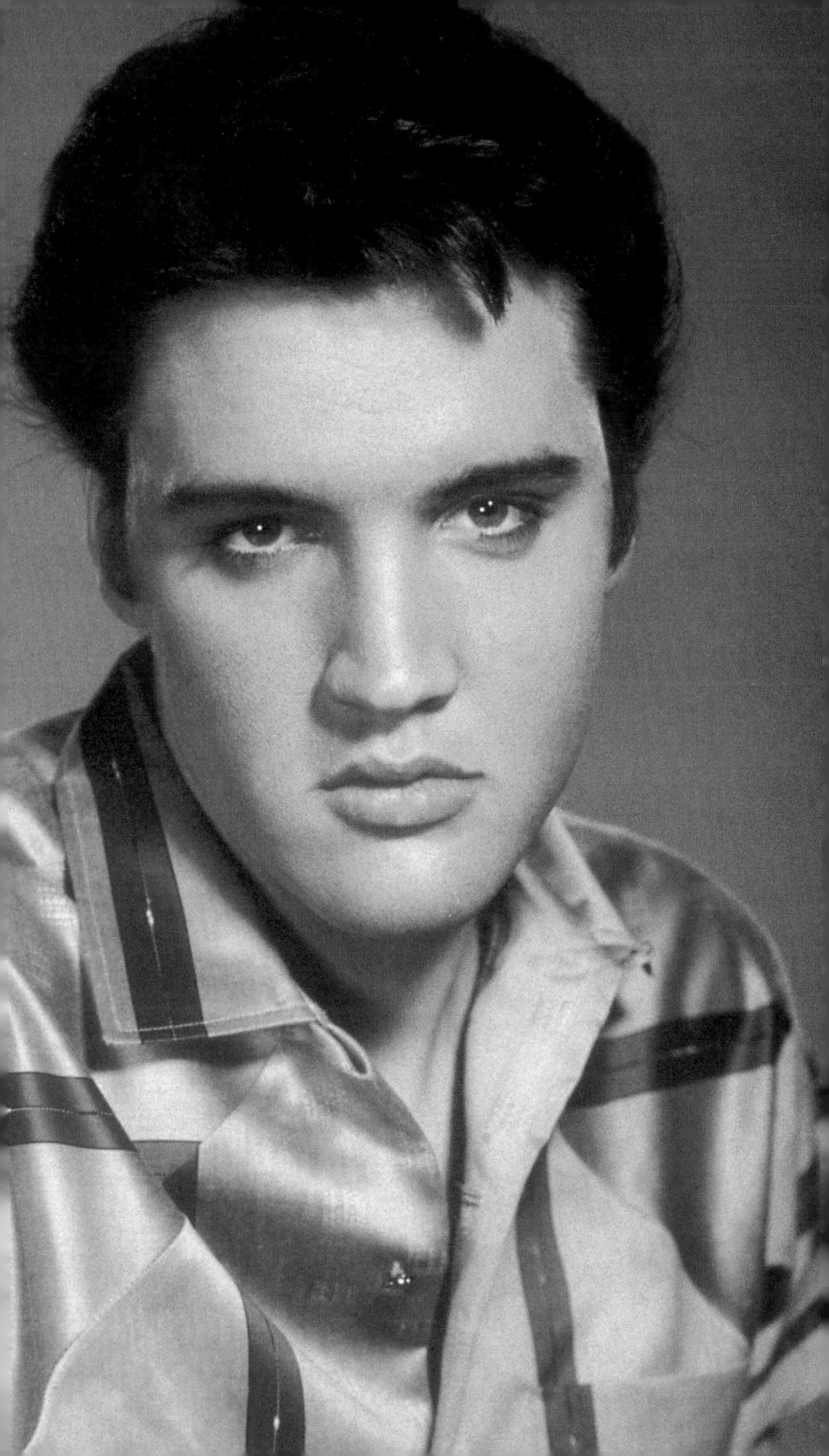

HEARTBREAK HOTEL
LOVE ME TENDER TOO MU

His Master's Pipe. The Colonel points out the fine print in his contract with a bored-looking Elvis.

HEARTBREAK

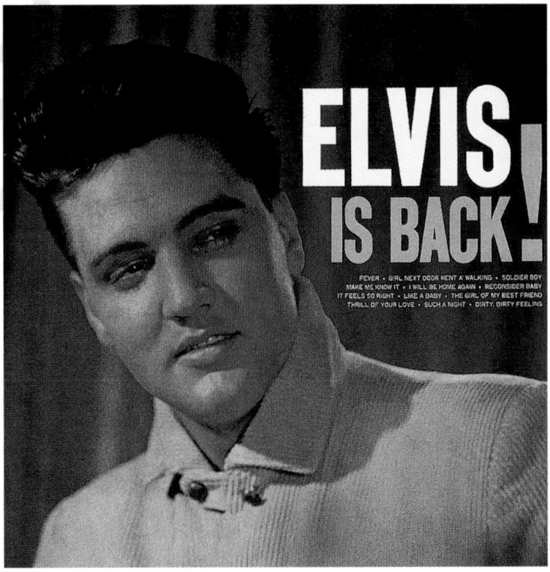

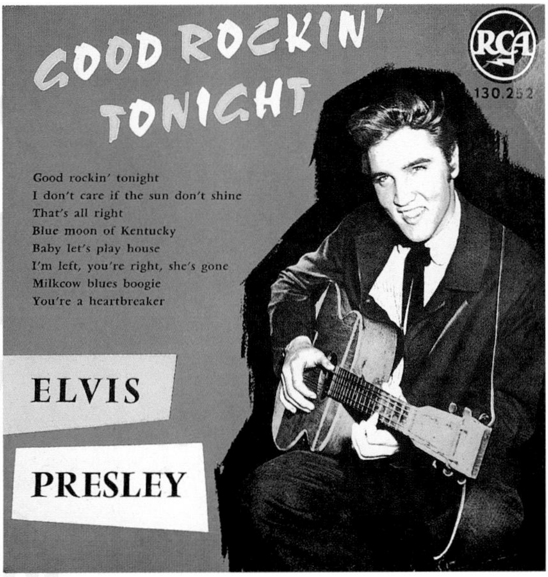

Left: The trademark Elvis smile-come-sneer and quiff.

Above, top: The title says it all. The first post-Army album.

Above: A French 10-inch mini-album release from the 1980s.

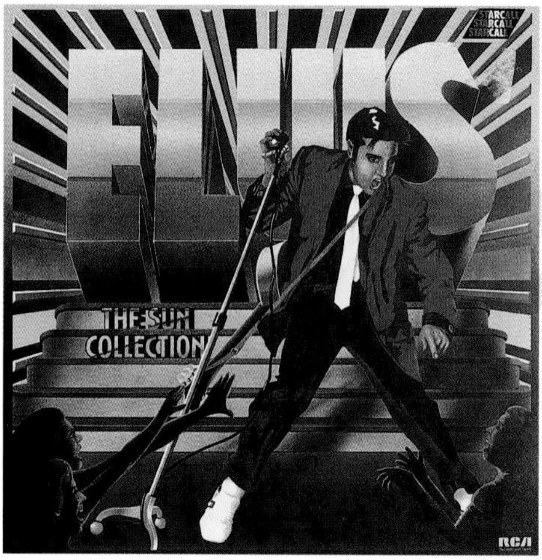

Right: The King returns. Elvis in full military regalia on returning to America from duty served in Germany.

Above, top: The sleeve of the Sun Sessions, compiled by NME's Roy Carr and released by RCA in 1976.

Above: The US Mail stamp produced in honour of Elvis. A vote among the American populace selected a 1950s image for the first issue.

PRESLE
FRS

Elvis at Graceland.

LOVE ME TENDER

TOO MUCH

WOODEN HEART

Left: The bride and groom with their towering wedding cake, the Aladdin Hotel, Las Vegas, Nevada, 1 May 1967.

Above: The happy family. Elvis and Priscilla smile while Lisa Marie can't look.

A BIG HUNK
OF LOVE
ALL SHOOK UP
TEDDY BEAR
HARD HEADED
WOMAN
ONE NIGHT
STUCK ON YOU
IT'S NOW OR
NEVER

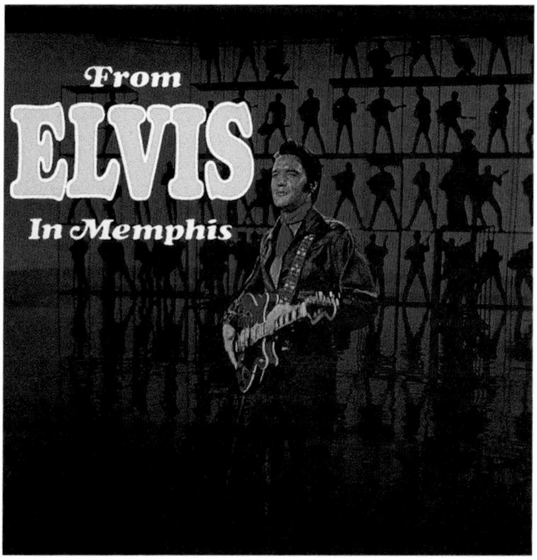

Left: Elvis on stage in his 1968 television comeback special broadcast. It was the first time that he had appeared wearing black leather. He wore the suit for the early part of the show to perform rock'n'roll songs.

Above: The sleeve for *From Elvis In Memphis.* Songs recorded after the success of the TV special, the album was released in June 1969. The cover image is taken from the broadcast.

Left: Elvis in action in the white-suited gospel section of the TV special.

Below: The original British sleeve for the *Elvis TV Special* album.

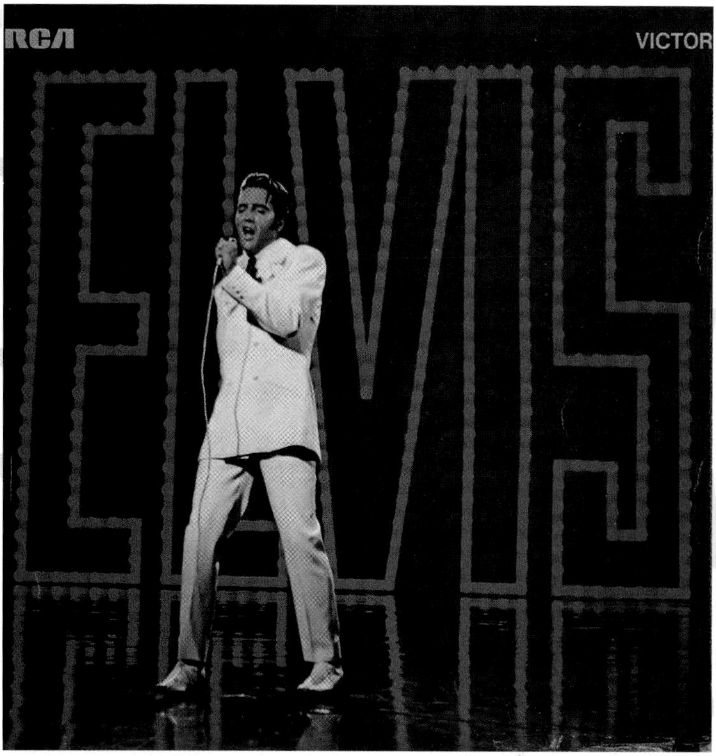

The A–Z of Elvis

J is for Jumpsuit

Costume designer Bill Belew was 37 when he got the call from the NBC network to work on Elvis' 1968 comeback special (see B is for Black Leather). Bill would remain as Elvis' personal costume carer until the end, making all of the stage wear and most of the King's personal wardrobe, too. Bill designed the first jumpsuit for the 1969 Las Vegas, International Hotel residency – it was white and he called it Shooting Stars. Bill also made a couple of two-piece, loose-fitting suits 'based on karate wear', because he'd noticed that the King was into karate. One was white and the other black – Elvis preferred the black but his fans liked the white. Elvis liked the jumpsuits because they offered him ease of movement, so Bill made them for the rest of the King's career. He stitched on different stones and adornments and later added bell-bottoms and stand-up collars (the latter because he was a long-time admirer of the Napoleonic era). The suits were all made from 100% wool gabardine in a process that Bill claimed 'only the Italians seemed to have mastered', and was chosen because ice skaters used the material. The studs on Elvis' jumpsuits were brass or silver, the rhinestones hand-picked by Bill on buying trips to Paris, although they were invariably made in Austria or Czechoslovakia. The jumpsuits were made either at Ice Capades Costumes or subsidiary International Costumes in Hollywood. Elvis rarely went to Bill for fittings and all the jumpsuits were made from previous measurements (which could explain why some would split on stage). The capes and engraved leather belts were usually Elvis' suggestion. He liked to wear them off stage, so figured that they'd look good on stage, too. The most impressive of all the jumpsuits worn by Elvis was probably the one made for the 1973 *Aloha from Hawaii* TV special. Elvis had asked for something that would say 'America' to the audience. Bill suggested the American Eagle and a gabardine legend was born. You can buy replicas of the King's jumpsuits plus authentic drawings of the original Elvis suits by Bill from B&K Enterprises, P.O. Box 2057, Clarksville, IN 47131-2057. B&K employ the embroidery services of Gene Doucette, Bill's assistant designer in the 70s. (Elvis impersonator Mike Memphis wore a B&K suit in the episode of *The Sopranos* in which he is whacked by Big Pussy.) You can find a directory of every jumpsuit Elvis wore on stage with dates and appearance times at http://elvisconcert.www6.50megs.com/jumpsuits.

The LP sleeve of special edition release 'Reconsider Baby', 1985. The album featured the original, uncensored version of One Night.

Elvis threw himself into this performance in the studio and after ten takes confessed himself satisfied with the way it sounded. Perhaps part of the no-nonsense appeal of 'One Night' comes from the absence of The Jordanaires – although their harmonies were undoubtedly flawless, they had tended to smooth out the rough edges of all Elvis' recent records.

At the beginning of 1959 as 'One Night' began its three-week run at No.1, Elvis was already out of sight, far away in Germany doing his military service – but back home in America, things were fast getting out of control in the rock'n'roll firmament. The flamboyant Little Richard had forsaken rock'n'roll for religion, and withdrawn from the limelight. Elvis' Sun labelmate Jerry Lee Lewis had only played three of the 35 dates on his 1958 UK tour before the press discovered that his new bride was his fourteen-year-old cousin. A full-blown scandal ensued, questions

'THERE WAS ALWAYS SOMETHING JUST BORDERING ON RUDENESS ABOUT ELVIS. HE NEVER ACTUALLY DID ANYTHING RUDE BUT HE ALWAYS SEEMED AS IF HE WAS JUST GOING TO. ON A SCALE OF ONE TO TEN, I WOULD RATE HIM ELEVEN'

Sammy Davis Jnr

were asked in Parliament, and Jerry Lee was hounded out of the country.

Back in America, Buddy Holly had already established himself as one of the prime movers of rock'n'roll. Buddy had been an enthusiastic member of the audience when Elvis had breezed through Lubbock, Texas just four years before, but by the age of 21 the myopic Holly had enjoyed big hits of his own, with classics like 'Oh Boy', 'Rave On', 'That'll Be The Day' and 'Peggy Sue' to his name. As the 50s drew to an end, his pioneering use of strings on 'It Doesn't Matter Anymore' would suggest something of a new direction for rock'n'roll; but by then Buddy himself was already gone, killed in a plane crash on 3 February 1959, along with The Big Bopper ('Chantilly Lace') and Ritchie Valens ('La Bamba').

'HE WAS WHITE, BUT HE SANG BLACK' Chet Atkins

Although he was serving abroad and therefore out of the public eye, 'One Night' had given fans a potent reminder of just how menacing and sexy Elvis was still capable of sounding. But there was no denying the fact that with Elvis away, rock'n'roll had entered the doldrums – and that lethargy would continue to dog it until the breakthrough of The Beatles half a decade later.

Of course, the period between Elvis' army service and the outbreak of Beatlemania did contain some great one-off singles – courtesy of Phil Spector and Berry Gordy to name but two; but the threat that rock'n'roll had posed since Elvis' breakthrough in 1956 now seemed strangely eviscerated. It became clear that Elvis' army haircut had taken away more than just his famous sideburns.

(NOW AND THEN THERE'S) A FOOL SUCH AS I

Written by William Trader

Recorded 10 June 1958 at RCA Studios, Nashville

Guitar: Chet Atkins, Hank Garland, Elvis Presley
Bass: Bob Moore
Drums: D.J. Fontana
Bongos: Buddy Harman
Piano: Floyd Cramer
Vocals: The Jordanaires

Released 10 March 1959

Elvis had been familiar with '(Now And Then There's) A Fool Such As I' since 1953, when Hank Snow enjoyed a country hit with the song, but it wasn't until 1958, at that all-night pre-Germany session in Nashville, that he finally got round to recording his own version.

The song marks something of a change of direction for Elvis. A bluesy guitar figure ushers in the song, but the first voice you hear is that of The Jordanaires' bass singer Ray Walker. When Elvis joins in, he sounds relaxed and effortlessly in control, but strangely vulnerable too, as if the worries of the outside world have finally intruded into the recording studio.

With 'A Fool Such As I', Elvis begins the process of easing himself out of the 50s, the decade he had dominated so convincingly. It was a long way from the nervy energy of 'Heartbreak Hotel' and 'Jailhouse Rock' – but still, unmistakably, Elvis.

'WITHOUT ELVIS, NONE OF US COULD HAVE MADE IT' Buddy Holly

Although recorded the previous year, the release of 'A Fool Such As I' coincided with the posthumous success of Buddy Holly's 'It Doesn't Matter Anymore', the two records confirming the less frenzied direction rock'n'roll seemed to be taking as the 50s drew to a close. The recently deceased Holly was just one in a long line of Elvis disciples, youngsters inspired by the king of rock'n'roll, who had begun their own careers emulating him – so it was ironic that 'A Fool Such As I' took over the UK No.1 slot from 'It Doesn't Matter Anymore'.

A rare, untouched, naturalistic pose, early 50s.

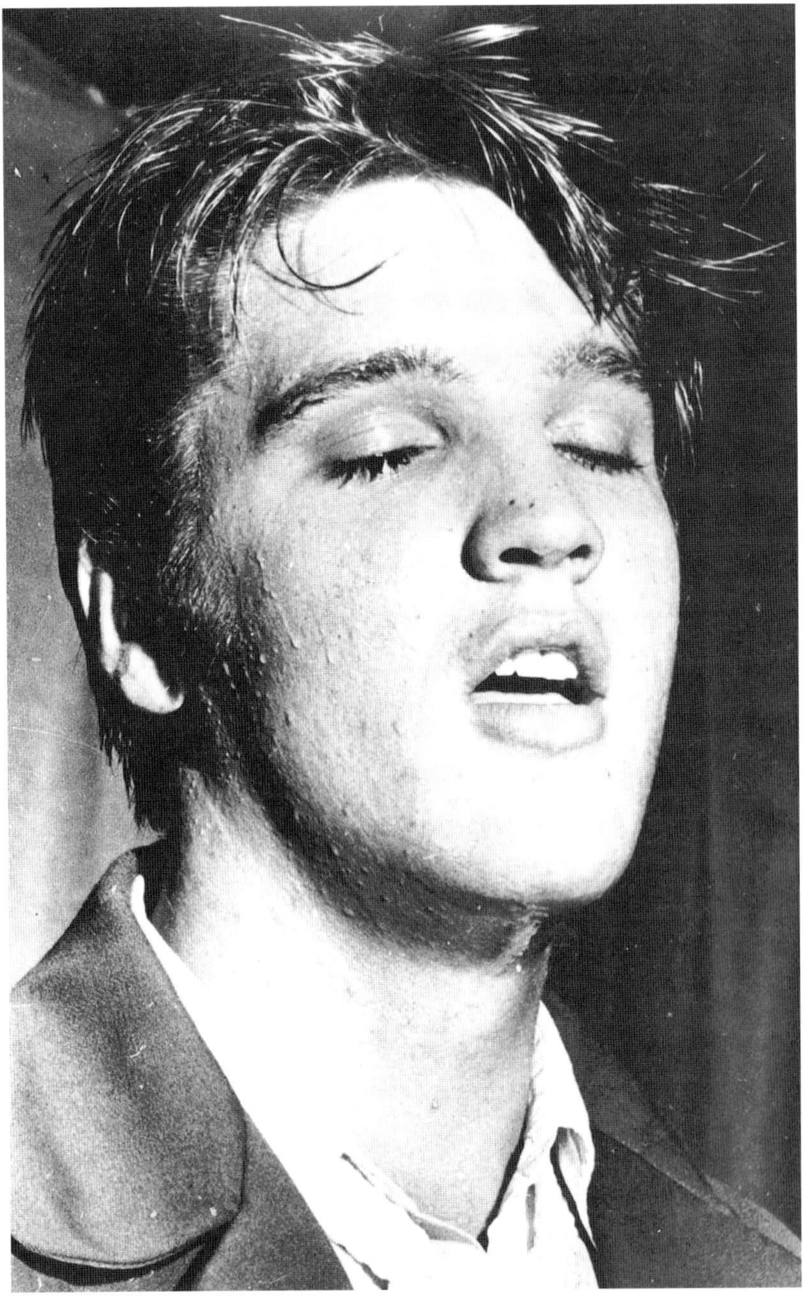

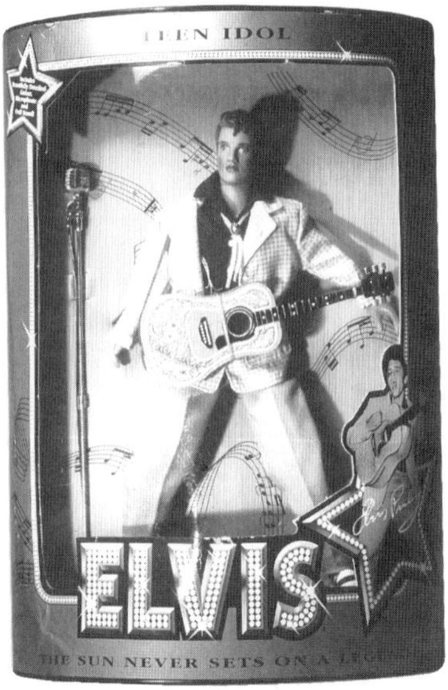

A 50s-era Graceland-approved Elvis doll of 1994.

Clearly, in Britain too, Elvis' conscription had signalled an enormous gap to be plugged. Cliff Richard was gaining a foothold on the charts, while Anthony Newley cashed in on Elvis' absence with the 1959 film *Idle On Parade*, a limp comedy with the engaging Newley cast as conscripted rock'n'roller 'Jeep Jones'. And despite the fact that the King still reigned at No.1 with 'A Fool Such As I', the lower rungs of the charts were already occupied by the mellower sounds of Frankie Vaughan's 'Come Softly To Me', Connie Francis with 'My Happiness' and Marty Wilde's 'Donna'.

As part of the Colonel's deliberate policy to remind fans of his boy, even though he was currently stationed far away in Europe, Elvis' version of 'A Fool Such As I' served its purpose on both sides of the Atlantic. In America the song took Elvis to No.2, even though the charts were now full of contenders like Paul Anka, Bobby Darin and Pat Boone, all of whom had made their mark – and none of whom had Uncle Sam disrupting their careers.

But as manager of the biggest star of the decade, Colonel Parker also had longer-term aims in mind: he was determined to help his boy mature from rock'n'roll rebel into an all-round entertainer. The move into movies had been phase one of that strategy; songs like 'A Fool Such As I' were just another step in the transition.

Eleven years later, 'A Fool Such As I' would be one of the two Elvis songs Bob Dylan chose to record as studio warm-ups for his *Self Portrait* album – the other was 'Can't Help Falling In Love'. As a teenager, Robert Zimmerman had revered Elvis; and the normally gravel-voiced Dylan went into crooning mode for his soft and sensitive cover. But although recorded in 1970, the tracks didn't surface until three years later, when both appeared on the potpourri album of outtakes, *Dylan (A Fool Such As I)*. It was also in 1970 – on *New Morning*, one of his many 'comeback' albums – that Dylan's 'Went To See The Gypsy' first appeared, a song widely believed to be about his only meeting with Elvis.

For Elvis, back in 1959, the success of smoother-edged material like 'A Fool Such As I', proved that he could plug the gap caused by his army exile. He may not have been immediately visible to his fans, but the continuing run of hits scored by the King across the water testified that Elvis was still very much in their hearts and minds.

The A–Z of Elvis

K is for Karate

Elvis first learned karate in the Army. He got his first black belt in Germany in 1960 and at the end of August 1974 received his eighth-degree black belt on stage in Vegas, dressed in full karate regalia. His karate skills seemed to give the King a sense of confidence and he'd often throw a pose in front of people whom he wanted to scare. During live performances in the 70s, rather than wiggle his hips, Elvis would throw karate poses and kicks in time to the music. He had numerous karate teachers on his payroll over the years, the most famous being ex-World Champion expert Mike Stone, the man whom Priscilla moved in with after leaving the King. Elvis once issued a hit order on Stone to his personal Mafia, seemingly unaware that they were not related in any way to the real Cosa Nostra. The hit never happened, as Elvis' step-brother David Stanley reports, though after issuing the order, Elvis 'required heavy sedation over the next few days before he calmed down'. According to David Stanley, two days before his final concert in June 1977, Elvis had performed his last great karate feat. He called for his limo to pull over at a gas station, leapt out and threw a few karate poses. 'If there's gonna be a fight,' he announced, 'it'll be with me.' Apparently he'd seen some men attacking the attendant and had gone in like a superhero. No blows were exchanged and everyone had their photograph taken with the King.

A BIG HUNK O' LOVE

Written by Aaron Schroeder, Sid Jaxon

Recorded 10 June 1958 at RCA Studios, Nashville

Guitar: Chet Atkins, Hank Garland, Elvis Presley
Bass: Bob Moore
Drums: D.J. Fontana
Piano: Floyd Cramer
Bongos: Buddy Harman
Vocals: The Jordanaires

Released 23 June 1959

This was to be Elvis' final No.1 of the 50s and, as his fans had come to expect, he went out with a bang. 'A Big Hunk O' Love' proved that, at the age of 24, he could still rock out with the best of the new breed when he wanted to. Elvis' performance was a timely reminder to those who had been captivated by the softer sound of 'A Fool Such As I' that he was still the king of rock'n'roll.

The song itself was rooted in the blues tradition that Elvis had grown to love while still a teenager in Memphis; and at the studio session Elvis was delighted with the hand-picked Nashville musicians like guitarists Chet Atkins and Hank Garland and electric bassist Bob Moore, who had been drafted in to replace the departed Scotty Moore and Bill Black. Floyd Cramer's piano hammers the message home – and vocally, Elvis sounds uncharacteristically out of control. But when the record was released, just a year later, it marked the end of an era in more ways than one.

Elvis was still exiled in Germany when 'A Big Hunk O' Love' was released, but this would be the final single released during his army service. It had been a big gamble as to whether his fans would be willing to wait. As it turned out, it was a gamble that paid off; but of course no one – not Elvis, not the Colonel, not RCA, not even his fans – knew that for certain at the time.

When Elvis went to Germany, he really did wonder if the world would still remember him at when he finished his two years' army service in 1960. His departure from America had been hysterical, marked by a press conference carefully orchestrated by the Colonel – who saw this as a perfect opportunity to plug the latest Presley product, *King Creole*. And there had been similar pandemonium when Elvis first arrived in Europe on 1 October 1958.

In Europe, rock'n'roll was still seen as a threat, a harbinger of doom – Bill Haley & The Comets'

A Big Hunk O' Love

Elvis poses for the publicity department, 1957.

concert appearances had ended in mayhem, as teenagers trashed the venues in homage to the kiss-curled avuncular one. Even screenings of *The Blackboard Jungle,* which featured Haley's 'Rock Around The Clock' on the soundtrack, frequently ended in riots. Buddy Holly's 1958 British dates had been a bit more sedate, but teenagers like John Lennon and Paul McCartney nevertheless sat mesmerised by his TV appearance, on *Sunday Night At The London Palladium,* literally watching Holly's every move.

It was hardly surprising then that the presence of Elvis Presley on the European mainland had sent the rumour factory into overtime. But despite substantial encouragement from the army authorities, Elvis didn't make a single concert appearance during his army spell. The closest he ever got was to sit at a piano in a Paris nightclub

A 1992-made Elvis wall clock. The legs swing like a pendulum in an approximation of 1950s-era Elvis.

while on leave in 1959 and sing 'Willow Weep For Me', but this was to be the first and last European performance of his life.

Private Presley's refusal to perform in public did nothing to prevent his German home becoming a shrine for European fans, who queued patiently in all weathers waiting for autographs and photographs. Among the pilgrims was another young rock'n'roller – known as 'the British Elvis' – who was accruing quite a reputation for himself back at home. Sadly though, when Cliff Richard called in at Bad Nauheim, Elvis wasn't at home.

In his off-duty hours in Germany, Elvis relaxed by playing the piano, listening to albums of gospel music and trying out songs on his newly purchased tape recorder – as ever, his repertoire consisted both of current rock'n'roll favourites and songs recalled from his youth. A brief selection of Elvis' 1959 home recordings from Germany can be found on the 1997 box-set *Platinum: A Life In Music.* Sitting in front of a piano at home in Bad Nauheim, with the tape rolling, Elvis coasts through 'I'll Take You Home Again Kathleen'; Tony Martin's 1949 hit 'There's No Tomorrow'; and 'April Strings', a song he declined to record, but which Cliff Richard did include on the B-side of his 1959 No.1 'Living Doll'.

RCA were still pressurising Elvis to come up with some new recordings – the label even suggested that he fly home to America during his army leave specifically to record. Elvis refused that offer, but he did spend time in Germany sifting through sheet music, considering songs that music publisher Freddy Bienstock wanted him to record as soon as he was safely back on American soil.

To keep the fans – and RCA – happy while his boy served out his time in the Army, the Colonel's 1959 Christmas present was Volume II of *Elvis' Golden*

Records, today best remembered for the outfit Elvis sported on the sleeve. The legendary gold suit – made by Nudie's of Hollywood – may have been unforgettable, but in the event it had a short life. Elvis soon discovered that it was incredibly uncomfortable to perform in, while the Colonel fretted because expensive flecks of gold paint flaked off every time Elvis flexed his legs.

Finally, after two years' army service, the newly promoted Sergeant Presley was discharged and free to resume his day job. He left Germany for America, uncertain of what lay ahead – and en route made his first, and only, visit to Britain.

US Army 53310761 Private Presley had glimpsed the White Cliffs of Dover on his way to military service in Germany, but the only time he actually made physical contact with British soil (well, tarmac really) was on the evening of Wednesday 2 March 1960, when the plane taking him back to the States landed to refuel at Prestwick International Airport on the west coast of Scotland. Elvis descended from the DC-7, signed autographs for an hour, is rumoured to have drunk a cup of tea, and commented: 'This is quite a country, I must see more of it.'

He never did. Despite the multi-million pound offers and heartfelt entreaties, for the rest of his life Elvis Presley never made a single appearance anywhere outside of the US.

The A–Z of Elvis

L is for Led Zeppelin

On 11 May 1974 Elvis played the Forum in Los Angeles to 18,500 in a late-afternoon concert. The same number turned up to the evening show, and among them were the four members of the biggest rock band in the world at that time, Led Zeppelin. David Stanley, in his *Elvis Encyclopedia*, states that he spotted them and told Elvis that they were there before the King went on for the late show. Elvis, says Stanley, played one of the best shows that he'd seen and when he came off stage simply said, 'I guess I showed them boys how to rock.' Unusually for Elvis at this time, he seemed to know of the group. (Elsewhere in the *Encyclopedia*, Stanley tells a story about introducing Elvis to Eric Clapton and the King not knowing who he was. 'And what do you do?' he'd asked.) As Stanley tells it the band then filed into Elvis' dressing room and stood around looking star-struck. 'I mean they were like little kids,' writes Stanley. When they were leaving Robert Plant turned in the door and sang in a perfect Elvis voice, 'Treat me like a fool', to which the King responded, singing, 'Treat me mean and cruel'. 'The scary thing,' writes Stanley, 'was that Plant sounded exactly like Elvis.'

STUCK ON YOU

Written by Aaron Schroeder, J. Leslie McFarland

Recorded 21 March 1960 at RCA Studios, Nashville

Guitar: Scotty Moore, Elvis Presley
Bass: Hank Garland, Bob Moore
Drums: D.J. Fontana, Buddy Harman
Piano: Floyd Cramer
Vocals: The Jordanaires

Released 23 March 1960

Stuck On You

Like a presidential hopeful on the campaign trail, immediately following his discharge from the Army Elvis took a cross-country journey by train from Washington to Memphis. At every stop the crowds gathered eagerly, anxious to catch a glimpse of the man who, until now, feared they might have forgotten all about him.

RCA, and the world, were salivating for new Elvis Presley material – and, as usual, Colonel Parker was keen to keep them guessing. But even the Colonel realised there was a lot riding on Elvis' first release since leaving the Army.

Secrecy surrounding the new Elvis release was so extreme that when it came to arranging the recording, the musicians were told they were being hired for a Jim Reeves session. Finally though, everyone assembled in the studio, where they would remain throughout that March night. Elvis started out by warming up on 'Soldier Boy' and Otis Blackwell's jaunty 'Make Me Know It', before sinking his teeth into 'A Mess Of Blues', the first song written for him by Doc Pomus and Mort Shuman, who were just beginning to make their mark as songwriters. But the next song that night was the big one. The new single. The song that RCA pressing plants across the world were waiting for: 'Stuck On You'.

Written by Aaron Schroeder – who had co-written Elvis' previous No.1, 'A Big Hunk O' Love', and would later pen 'It's Now Or Never' – 'Stuck On You' was a near-relation to 'All Shook Up', catchy, but without the dark menace of, say, 'Heartbreak Hotel'. This was a foretaste of the Elvis that the world would come to know and love throughout much of the ensuing decade – the Elvis who would enchant and entice on 'It's Now Or Never', 'Are You Lonesome Tonight?' and 'Wooden Heart'.

Such was the anticipated demand for the new record that sleeves were printed up and ready to go even before RCA knew what the single would be. The picture sleeve promised 'Elvis' 1st new recording for his 50,000,000 fans all over the world'. Within 48 hours of its recording, a million copies of 'Stuck On You' had been inserted into their sleeves and were on sale in the stores.

Issued in 1997, this beautiful calendar uses images reprinted from photographer Wertheimer's book, *Elvis '56*.

Thanks to the Colonel's careful planning, Elvis was given an unrivalled opportunity to plug 'Stuck On You'. In 1957 Frank Sinatra had raged against rock'n'roll, calling it 'the most brutal, ugly, degenerate, vicious form of expression – lewd, sly, in plain fact, dirty – a rancid smelling aphrodisiac.' Three years later, Sinatra would welcome the man who personified the music he so despised as his guest. Colonel Parker had secured Elvis a one-off appearance on Sinatra's keenly anticipated 1960 TV spectacular, for an equally spectacular and previously unheard-of fee: $125,000. It was a perfect opportunity for the nation to say: 'Welcome Back Elvis'.

'MY CRUSHING AMBITION IN LIFE WAS TO BE AS BIG AS ELVIS PRESLEY' John Lennon

Despite the loss of those trademark sideburns, and the extra pounds gained thanks to army chow, it was a remarkable return. Even before it was released, 'Stuck On You' had racked up advance sales of 1,275,077 copies in America alone – the biggest pre-release sales for any single prior to The Beatles. As the title of his first post-army album triumphantly announced: *Elvis Is Back!*

The album too was exemplary, in fact it was one of the best collections of songs Elvis ever released. He recreated Peggy Lee's 'Fever' as a virtually solo,

Elvis left the Army with the rank of Sergeant. 1960.

sultry, finger-clicking masterpiece of economy; he covered contemporary pop on 'The Girl Of My Best Friend' and 'The Girl Next Door Went A'Walking'; got downright dirty on Johnny Ray's 'Such A Night'; and wound the whole thing up with a storming take on Lowell Fulson's 'Reconsider Baby'.

The triple whammy of the single, the Sinatra TV special, and the *Elvis Is Back!* album, saw the King regain his crown convincingly. But there were changes written on the wind and a new cast was already limbering up in the wings, ready to take on the 60s. Names like Dylan, Jagger, Lennon and McCartney may have been unknown as the decade began, but by the time it ended, they would have all but eclipsed that of Elvis Presley.

In the two years during which Elvis had been away on duty, a whole host of lesser talents had plugged the gap in his homeland. Rock'n'roll had been further emasculated by Chuck Berry's imprisonment on morals charges in 1959 and a car crash in 1960 that caused Eddie Cochran's death and injured Gene Vincent. American teenagers now stared at pin-up pictures of the likes of Frankie Avalon, Fabian and Bobby Rydell – and they flocked to buy their records too.

Just five months after Elvis Presley flew home from Germany in March 1960, The Beatles made their first appearances in Hamburg. The times they were indeed a-changin' …

The A–Z of Elvis

M is for Memphis Mafia

The collective name given to the bunch of local Memphis guys who acted as Elvis' bodyguards, babysitters, drug procurers, girl-getters, mates and car-buyers. Among the first to live, travel and play with Elvis were the West brothers – Sonny and Red – Joe Esposito, Charlie Hodge and Lamar Fike. Over the years they were joined on the payroll by the Stanley brothers – Ricky, Billy and David – Jerry Schilling, Larry Geller, Marty Lacker, Dave Hebler and numerous others. Three of the Mafia wrote the first exposé book on Elvis. Red and Sonny West and Dave Hebler's *Elvis: What Happened?* published in 1977, just months after they'd been fired by Vernon Presley, was the first book to carry allegations of the King's drug taking and his erratic mental and physical health. Elvis was devastated by its publication. He'd even offered the publishers money not to go ahead with it. For Vernon the book was proof of his long-held distrust and dislike not just of those three but of the whole of the Memphis Mafia, whom he felt exercised an unhealthy influence over his son. But then, the Colonel was nearer Vernon's age. In truth various members of the Memphis Mafia had, over the years, played vital roles in keeping the King's numerous dirty secrets out of the public eye. A couple of them had been arrested with false prescriptions attempting to collect drugs for Elvis, quite a few had taken physical hits in the service of protecting Elvis and none were paid more than $500 a week. For that they were often shouted at, abused and belittled by the King when he felt like it – which happened more and more often as he neared the undignified end of his life. Red and Sonny West, who had known him almost all his life, claimed with some justification that publishing their book was a last-ditch attempt at making him and the whole world aware of what danger he was putting himself in by taking so many uppers and downers. They had angrily confronted Elvis about his drug usage during the last years that they were in his employ, to little effect. Unfortunately the book also failed to stir Elvis into cleaning up his act.

IT'S NOW OR NEVER

Written by Eduardo di Capua, Aaron Schroeder, Wally Gold

Recorded 3 April 1960 at RCA Studios, Nashville

Guitar: Scotty Moore, Hank Garland, Elvis Presley
Bass: Bob Moore
Drums: D.J. Fontana, Buddy Harman
Piano: Floyd Cramer
Saxophone: Boots Randolph
Vocals: The Jordanaires

Released 5 July 1960

It's Now Or Never

Less than two weeks later, in early April 1960, Elvis was back in Nashville for his second post-army recording session. Besides recording the bulk of the album *Elvis Is Back!*, he also found time to cut two consecutive No.1 singles, the first of which was 'It's Now Or Never'.

Based upon 'O Sole Mio', an Italian operatic standard written in 1901 and popularised by Caruso, the song's melody had long been a favourite of Elvis'. He had probably first become familiar with the tune when it was revived by Mario Lanza, one of his favourite singers while growing up; but while visiting Elvis on service in Germany, music publisher Freddy Bienstock had also heard him singing 'There's No Tomorrow', an English version of the song that had been a 1949 hit for Tony Martin.

Sensing Elvis' fondness for the melody and in anticipation of the post-army Presley career, on his return to America Bienstock commissioned some new English words for the song. Elvis was captivated by 'It's Now Or Never'. He recognised the challenge it posed to him as a singer, particularly in its operatic conclusion, and he identified with the drama of the new lyrics, appreciating that this song could bring him to an even wider audience than before.

Once again, Elvis' instincts proved to be impeccable. 'It's Now Or Never' went on to become the best-selling Presley single ever, with estimated worldwide sales in excess of 20 million. It also proved one of Elvis' enduring favourites, apparently replacing 'Don't Be Cruel' as the pick of his own hits.

The significance of the single was immediately apparent: 'It's Now Or Never' gave Elvis a whole new audience in America, with many easy listening stations playing a Presley single for the very first time. Coming on the back of his army service, Elvis was now gaining a new, more respectable image, as a clean-cut young American who had served his country with pride. With perfect timing,

'It's Now Or Never' also reached out afresh to Elvis' original audience – the teenagers who had first screamed for him in 1956 were now well on their way to adulthood.

Plate 2 in a limited edition by Diane Sivavec, this ornamental plate is titled 'Tupelo Mississippi' and was issued in 1992. It shows Elvis in front of the shack he was born in.

In Britain too, 'It's Now Or Never' took on a life of its own. Because of copyright problems relating to 'O Sole Mio', the UK release of 'It's Now Or Never' was delayed for three months, but when it was eventually released in Britain in late October 1960, sales were phenomenal. One record shop in London closed its doors on the first Saturday of release to everyone except those wishing to buy the new Elvis single. It didn't take long for 'It's Now Or Never' to become Elvis' most successful British hit: it entered the charts immediately at No.1, where it remained for an unrivalled eight straight weeks, until knocked off the top by 'the British Elvis', Cliff Richard, with his fourth No.1, 'I Love You'.

'EVERYTIME I FELT LOW, I JUST PUT ON AN ELVIS RECORD AND I'D FEEL GREAT'

Paul McCartney

The only act ever to approach Elvis Presley's success was The Beatles, who broke open the American market in 1964 and dominated the pop landscape for the remainder of the 60s. All four Beatles were major-league Elvis fans, and at the start of their career the group would usually include a number of Presley songs in their stage set.

The release of *The Beatles Live At The BBC* in 1994 provided a vital missing link in the group's history – here were the songs they would perform in Liverpool and Hamburg, in the years before the roar of the crowd drowned out their voices and they began to have confidence in their own material. Sure enough, the Elvis music that had inspired them as teenagers was well represented – 'I Got A Woman', 'That's All Right, Mama', 'I'm Gonna Sit Right Down And Cry (Over You)' and 'I Forgot To Remember To Forget'.

Elvis relaxes.

Once the Lennon and McCartney songwriting juggernaut got underway, cover versions rarely got a look in on Beatle albums. But, intriguingly, when John Lennon released his 1975 *Rock 'N' Roll* album, a homage to the music that had inspired him as a kid, the music of Elvis Presley was conspicuous by its absence – even though he had previously gone on record as a serious fan, saying quite simply: 'Before Elvis, there was nothing.'

Paul McCartney, on the other hand, has gone out of his way to pay tribute to the influence Elvis had on him. On Wings' first tour in 1972, 'Blue Moon Of Kentucky' was a staple of their set, and the same song found its way on to Paul's 1991 *Unplugged* album, along with another Elvis favourite from the Sun years, 'Good Rockin' Tonight'. In 1988, *The Russian Album* found room for McCartney's pounding take on 'That's All Right, Mama'; and two years later he revisited the Elvis legacy again when he joined a host of other famous fans on *The Last Temptation Of Elvis*, a tribute album imaginatively compiled by *NME*'s Roy Carr in aid of the Nordoff-Robbins music charity. 'It's Now Or Never' was the song Paul chose to record for *The Last Temptation Of Elvis*, and he was in good company, singing alongside the likes of Robert Plant ('Let's Have A Party'), The Pogues ('Got A Lot Of Livin' To Do'), Hall and Oates ('Can't Help Falling In Love') and Bruce Springsteen ('Viva Las Vegas'). A couple of years ago when McCartney revisited classic rock'n'roll on the album *Run Devil Run*, he unwound by including three songs popularised by Presley – 'All Shook Up', 'I Got Stung' and 'Party'.

One sunny summer's day I sat down and asked the former Beatle about his memories of Elvis, the 50s, rock'n'roll, and life before The Beatles. It soon became obvious that all McCartney's memories of the period were coloured by the unforgettable impact of rock'n'roll: 'For all of us who love rock'n'roll, it's the beginning, the beginning of it all, the first thrill. It's like the first time you ever made love, it just never goes away.

'There are a lot of songs I would like to do of Elvis',' McCartney continued. 'The choice this time, I didn't really think about it too much, other than what came into my head. I remember George and I hitch-hiked to Harlech in Wales, and we had *Elvis Golden Records: Volume I* on that whole week. So anything off that I'd love to do.

'We didn't want to go to Vegas, it could only have been a disappointment. But meeting him was nice. We had a good time. It was great. We were all very pleased to meet him, and he was a great, a real good guy, in very good shape. It was before his crazed period. He was really cool to us. We just sat in awe. We had a great evening. I'm really glad to have met him.'

The A–Z of Elvis

N is for Narc

Elvis dressed like a superhero when he went to meet President Nixon on 21 December 1970. Somewhere in his prescription-addled brain he probably believed that he, the Caped Narc, could rid America of its drug problems with help only from his Memphis Mafia. Elvis liked to collect police badges, and particularly narcotics officer badges. He gave them out to his Mafia and attempted to employ the two youngest Stanley brothers as his undercover agents at their high school. David Stanley claims that he was stoned on cannabis at the time his big half-brother tried to recruit him. After Elvis' death, Nixon stated that, 'Elvis wanted to be an example to young people. Some say that because he used drugs, he couldn't. But they overlooked the fact that he never used illegal drugs. The drugs were always prescribed by his physician. He was a very sincere and decent man.' It was a poor attempt to clear himself of accusations that he wanted the photo opportunity with the biggest star in the country, despite FBI memos stating that Elvis was psychologically addicted to cocaine. The same memo goes on to say that Elvis had turned down an offer to tour England worth several million dollars 'for fear that he would be caught in possession of or using narcotics in a foreign country'. Which suggests that his being a narc offered the King enough protection to carry on with his drug abuse in the US.

ARE YOU LONESOME TONIGHT?

Written by Roy Turk, Lou Handman

Recorded 4 April 1960 at RCA Studios, Nashville

Guitar: Scotty Moore, Hank Garland, Elvis Presley
Bass: Bob Moore
Drums: D.J. Fontana, Buddy Harman
Piano: Floyd Cramer
Saxophone: Boots Randolph
Vocals: The Jordanaires

Released 2 November 1960

Over the years Colonel Tom Parker had guided Elvis from his beginnings in smoky honky-tonks and fairgrounds to rock'n'roll infamy, celluloid success, and beyond. He had negotiated all the concert contracts, wrung every last cent out of RCA and grappled with film studios to get the very best deal for his boy. As he was fond of saying: 'When I first knew Elvis he had a million dollars' worth of talent. Now he has a million dollars.'

The Colonel was great at taking care of business – that was a given. But many were mystified by some of the decisions he made about his boy's career, particularly his refusal to allow Elvis to perform in Europe or Asia – or, indeed, anywhere outside North America. From early on, it was assumed that Parker's military title was bogus – although both Elvis and Parker were later made honorary colonels – but it was not until much later that his real reason for keeping Elvis in America became apparent. Colonel Thomas Andrew Parker had, in fact, been born Andreas Cornelis van Kuijk in Breda, Holland and his true status in America was that of an illegal Dutch immigrant.

In November 1961 *Melody Maker* devoted its front page to the headline: 'Elvis For Britain', but we know now that however much Elvis may have wished to tour – and there are strong indications

'I HOPE THAT NOBODY WILL EVER FORGET HOW HE INFLUENCED US ALL – HE ISN'T JUST A HISTORICAL PHENOMENON, BUT RATHER SOMETHING VERY LASTING' Roy Orbison

The well-greased quiff and sultry stare of an international sex god. 1960.

that following his army stint, he was keen to play in Europe – there was no way he could have worked abroad. The singer simply wouldn't have gone without his manager, and his manager could never leave America, for fear of not being allowed back in.

It wasn't always an easy relationship. Elvis appreciated what the Colonel had accomplished for him, but as his dreams of a worthwhile acting career were replaced by the reality of a Tinseltown treadmill on which he churned out mindless movies he had lost all interest in, Elvis began increasingly to resent the Colonel's narrow-minded vision of where his career was heading.

In spring 1960, however, all was still well between the King and the Colonel. And so it was that early on the morning of 4 April, in a Nashville recording studio, with one No.1 already in the bag, Elvis acquiesced to the Colonel's request to record a specific song. It was to be the only time in his career that Elvis would ever defer to Colonel Parker on a musical matter. The recording took place in the early hours, but not until the lights had been dimmed at Elvis' request, to help him strike just the right intimate note on 'Are You Lonesome Tonight?'.

The Colonel's wife Marie (after whom Elvis' daughter Lisa Marie would later be named) had a fondness for the ballad, which had first been a hit in 1927 for one Henry Burr. Al Jolson had also recorded it, but it was the hit version cut by crooner Gene Austin in the 40s, while Colonel Parker was his agent, that led to the Parkers' fondness for the song.

'Are You Lonesome Tonight?' ploughed the same successful furrow as 'It's Now Or Never', presenting an intimate, more mature-sounding Elvis. Much of the song's appeal came from the unusual spoken-word interlude (based on Act II, Scene VII of Shakespeare's *As You Like It*: 'all the world's a stage …'), which gave the impression that Elvis was talking to you – directly, and in person.

Inevitably, 'Are You Lonesome Tonight?' inspired a flood of 'answer' records, including no fewer than four female versions of 'Yes, I'm Lonesome Tonight'.

The song became one of his most popular hits and when he returned to the concert stage nearly a decade later, Elvis was honour-bound to include it in performance, but he always had difficulties keeping a straight face during the recitation section. A 'laughing version' of 'Are You Lonesome Tonight?' – featuring Elvis cracking up and ad-libbing during the quiet bit – was released in 1982, and reached No.25 on the British charts.

For most fans though, the original 1960 'Are You Lonesome Tonight?' remains the perennial favourite. In Britain the song took a month to reach No.1, and confirmed the singer's continued domination of the UK chart. 'Are You Lonesome Tonight?' was the second of twelve consecutive Presley single releases in the UK – ten of which made No.1. From the very beginning of the 60s, right up until the breakthrough of The Beatles three years later, Elvis Presley was pre-eminent in the recorded music scene in Britain. Thanks to quality material, canny marketing and a regular supply of colourful films for his fans, Elvis' position as the king of pop appeared unassailable.

The A–Z of Elvis

O is for Oh, Mama

Elvis' relationship with his mother has been the subject of many thousands of words from biographers, academics and psychologists around the world over the past three decades. However, none of them have ever come remotely as close to capturing the essence of the King and his Mama as a 2-D figure whose escapades are required viewing on the Cartoon Network for any and all Elvis fans. 'Oh Mama' is the catch phrase of Johnny Bravo, a cartoon character who sounds uncannily like Elvis, lives with his mother and is sorely deluded about the effect that his massive chest, huge blond quiff, dark glasses and karate poses has upon 'purty gurls'. Whenever Johnny Bravo sees a young, curvy female he immediately throws supersonic speed karate shapes. Invariably the girl rejects him as nastily as she can, to which Johnny utters 'Oh Mama! She wants me.' The bane of his life is the small girl who lives next door to Johnny and his mother. She loves him as only a small girl can, in what could possibly be a passing reference to the King's relationship with his only daughter, Lisa Marie.

WOODEN HEART

Written by Kay Twomey, Fred Wise, Ben Weisman, Bert Kaempfert

Recorded 28 April 1960 at RCA Studios, Hollywood

Guitar: Scotty Moore, Tiny Timbrell, Neal Matthews Jr, Elvis Presley
Bass: Ray Siegel
Drums: D.J. Fontana, Frank Bode, Bernie Mattinson
Piano: Dudley Brooks
Accordion: Jimmie Haskell
Vocals: The Jordanaires

Release: 24 February 1961 (UK only)

Wooden Heart

'Wooden Heart' gave Elvis his seventh British No.1, and made him the first act in the history of the British charts to score three consecutive No.1 singles.

This was his second British No.1 of 1961 and by the end of the year he had spent no less than 18 weeks at the top of the UK charts with four different songs. No other act before had ever enjoyed four No.1s in the space of a single year – but just to prove it wasn't a fluke, Elvis did it again the following year.

In Germany too the song was hugely successful, selling over a million copies in that country alone. But despite its enormous popularity in Europe, Elvis' 'Wooden Heart' was not released as a single in America until 1964, when it failed to reach even the lower reaches of the Top 40. In the wake of the song's European success, Joe Dowell jumped in and covered it for the American market, thereby stealing Elvis' thunder and adding his own name to that long list of one-hit wonders. Dowell's version of 'Wooden Heart' was recorded in a three-hour session in Nashville, and reached No.1 for one week only in August 1961.

Adapted by Kay Twomey, Fred Wise, Ben Weisman and Bert Kaempfert, from the German folk song 'Muss I Denn', 'Wooden Heart' was recorded for the soundtrack of *G.I. Blues*. His co-writing credit on 'Wooden Heart' had put Bert Kaempfert into the Presley firmament – but, ironically, just a month before 'Wooden Heart' was released in Britain, their paths crossed again when Kaempfert's instrumental hit 'Wonderland By Night' gave him an American No.1 – and in the process knocked Elvis' 'Are You Lonesome Tonight?' off the top spot. Kaempfert went on to even greater success and within five years would occupy a unique position in the history of popular music.

Born in Hamburg in 1923, Kaempfert was a songwriter, arranger and record producer; and three months after 'Wooden Heart' reached No.1 in

Britain, Kaempfert found himself back in a studio in his home town overseeing the first recording session by a Liverpool group called The Beatles. In the summer of 1966, Bert Kaempfert was at No.1 again, via an original tune of his, to which English lyrics had been added, this time recorded by Frank Sinatra. 'Strangers In The Night' became an American and British No.1, and in the process gave Bert Kaempfert the unique distinction of having been involved in the careers of the three biggest-selling acts in the history of popular music.

An original UK pressing of 'Wooden Heart'.

The success of *G.I. Blues*, Elvis' first post-army film, was undeniable – it became one of the top-grossing films of 1960 and the soundtrack reached No.1 on both sides of the Atlantic. But, popular success notwithstanding, Elvis himself was beginning to grow unhappy with the direction his career was taking – and he was particularly concerned about the low calibre of material that had filled the soundtrack this time around. Jerry Leiber and Mike Stoller had originally been asked to supply material, but by refusing to agree to Elvis taking a share of the publishing royalty, they had talked themselves out of the gig.

'ELVIS IS THE GREATEST BLUES SINGER IN THE WORLD TODAY' Joe Cocker

Elvis did have high hopes for his next film, *Wild In The Country*, in which he was to play a non-singing role. But the Colonel wasn't happy and, in the absence of a soundtrack album, neither were the fans. Thus, soon after its release the movie was recut to include four token songs. So it was back onto the Hollywood merry-go-round again, with Elvis locked into three films each and every year.

SURRENDER

Written by Doc Pomus and Mort Shuman

Recorded 30 October 1960 at RCA Studios, Nashville

Guitar: Scotty Moore, Hank Garland, Elvis Presley
Bass: Bob Moore
Drums: D.J. Fontana, Buddy Harman
Piano: Floyd Cramer
Saxophone: Boots Randolph
Vocals: The Jordanaires

Released 7 February 1961

'Are You Lonesome Tonight?' had proved the appeal of Elvis the balladeer and the success of 'It's Now Or Never' had confirmed the demand for a light operatic Elvis – no surprise then that his next No.1 should be cut from much the same cloth.

Once again it was music publisher Freddy Bienstock who recognised the hit potential of the 1911 Neapolitan standard 'Torna A Sorrento' ('Come Back To Sorrento'). The song had been recorded earlier by Dean Martin but, as with 'It's Now Or Never', Bienstock commissioned new English lyrics for Elvis to sing. Doc Pomus and Mort Shuman never met Elvis – they wrote and demoed material, which then went through a long and circuitous route to get to the King – but at least Elvis got to sing their songs.

There was no denying the success of 'Surrender', which gave Elvis another American and British No.1. But he was now 26 years old – and, in some eyes, more Tinseltown star than rock'n'roll legend. In a desperate effort to break the run of forgettable Hollywood fodder, both the singer and, uncharacteristically, his manager, were keen for Elvis to star as Hank Williams in the biopic *Your Cheatin' Heart*.

The project was green-lighted for early 1961, until the Colonel realised belatedly that, as the entire soundtrack consisted of Elvis singing Hank's songs, there was literally nothing in it for him. So the movie was shelved, although it was eventually filmed three years later, with George Hamilton starring as Hank – and Elvis did go on to record two classic Williams titles, 'Your Cheatin' Heart' and 'I'm So Lonesome I Could Cry'.

It was also in 1961 that Elvis gave his last live shows for eight long years. The Colonel had organised two charity concerts, one in Memphis, and one in Hawaii. The Memphis show marked Elvis' first live appearance for three years (a local

Surrender

'ELVIS WAS THE KING OF ROCK'N'ROLL BECAUSE HE WAS THE EMBODIMENT OF ITS SINS AND VIRTUES, GRAND AND VULGAR, RUDE AND ELEGANT, POWERFUL AND FRUSTRATED, ABSURDLY SIMPLE AND AWESOMELY COMPLEX'

Dave Marsh

reporter noted that he 'grabbed the mike as if he were trying to eat it') and the set-list included all the early pre-army material ('Hound Dog', 'Heartbreak Hotel', 'All Shook Up') as well as a résumé of his more recent hits ('Such A Night', 'Are You Lonesome Tonight?', 'It's Now Or Never').

The Hawaii show in March was planned to maximise publicity for Elvis' new movie, *Blue Hawaii* – but this time there was an element of altruism involved too. When the Colonel had learned there was a problem raising money to build a memorial for the men who died on the USS *Arizona* when it was sunk during the attack on Pearl Harbor in December 1941, the decision was made to donate proceeds from Elvis' show to the appeal. In all other respects, the Hawaii benefit was similar to the Memphis show, except that the evening was peppered with Hawaiian songs in recognition of the location – and, of course, in homage to Elvis' film.

The Colonel reckoned that with his difficulties in leaving America preventing Elvis from touring, the best way to appease his boy's fans worldwide was to keep them supplied with a regular stream of movies. Better still, three films a year

A UK original single version of 'Surrender'.

Elvis strumming between takes on the set of *Flaming Star*, 1961.

meant three soundtrack albums – and that should be enough to keep everyone happy. Quantity, not quality, was now quite clearly the philosophy.

Still, no-one could have guessed as Elvis quit the stage in Hawaii that the next time he would appear before a concert audience would be in July 1969.

The A–Z of Elvis

P is for Priscilla

Priscilla Beaulieu Presley is perhaps now best known for her roles in the string of *Naked Gun* movies in which she co-starred alongside Leslie Nielsen in the 90s. In the 80s she was a surprise member of the cast of big-shouldered soap *Dallas*. Today she is the chief executive of Elvis Presley Enterprises Inc by dint of the fact that she was Elvis' ex-wife and mother to his only officially recognised child, Lisa Marie. For a brief period in 1959 she was pure jailbait to Private Elvis Presley. The step-daughter of a US Army Captain, she so impressed Elvis that he gave her a solid gold and diamond-encrusted watch for Christmas that year. The next Yuletide holiday, with Elvis discharged, he persuaded the parents of the then fifteen-year old Priscilla that she'd be safe and permanently chaperoned during a long stay at his mansion in Memphis. Elvis was almost 26 years old at the time. The pair were engaged at Christmas 1966 and married in Las Vegas on 1 May 1967. Apparently Elvis didn't like Priscilla's plain white dress. Maybe that was why he continued to have sex with any woman who asked him (and a lot did) throughout their marriage. Exactly nine months to the day after the wedding, Lisa Marie was born, on 1 February 1968. Just four years later Priscilla and Lisa Marie left Graceland and moved to Marina del Ray. Elvis would later discover that former karate champion Mike Stone had moved in with them (see K is for Karate). Priscilla allowed Elvis unlimited access to Lisa Marie the whole time Stone, a former male model named Michael Edwards, was living there. Of course he wrote a book about their life together after they split up. But by then, Priscilla had written her own book about her life with Elvis, titled *Elvis And Me* (1985). The book was made into a television mini-series starring Susan Walters as Priscilla. Priscilla is credited with putting the affairs of EPE into order and making the kind of money out of her dead ex-husband that the Colonel could have done if he were capable when the cash cow was alive. Priscilla gave a warm eulogy at the memorial ceremony for Colonel Tom in 1997.

(MARIE'S THE NAME) HIS LATEST FLAME

Written by Doc Pomus and Mort Shuman

Recorded 26 June 1961 at RCA Studios, Nashville

Guitar: Scotty Moore, Hank Garland, Neal Matthews
Bass: Bob Moore
Drums: D.J. Fontana, Buddy Harman
Piano: Floyd Cramer
Saxophone: Boots Randolph
Vocals: The Jordanaires

Released 8 August 1961

With *Blue Hawaii* under his belt, shooting for *Follow That Dream* underway, and *Kid Galahad* ready on the blocks, 1961 was another typical year in Elvis' life. He may have grumbled about the sub-standard songs submitted for the soundtracks of his 60s' films, but he nevertheless went ahead and recorded them. Although, just occasionally – more by luck than by dint of the judgement that had served him so well during the 50s – a real cracker sneaked in under the ropes.

'(Marie's The Name) His Latest Flame' came to Elvis courtesy, once again, of the Brooklyn songwriters Doc Pomus and Mort Shuman – but only after it had been rejected by Bobby Vee. Mort Shuman later confessed that it was a Bo Diddley riff that had sparked the idea for 'His Latest Flame' but, Bo Diddley or not, '(Marie's The Name) His Latest Flame' is undeniably one of Elvis' finest post-army singles.

Powered by an unforgettable acoustic guitar riff, 'His Latest Flame' certainly owes a debt to Bo Diddley, but it also suggests something of a flamenco flourish. Floyd Cramer's piano lends an edge, while Elvis manages to exude bravura confidence. This song also has the distinction of being one of the very few Presley songs that his namesake, Elvis Costello, would later cover in concert.

The LP sleeve artwork for the third greatest hits package which features '(Marie's The Name) His Latest Flame'.

One of the great pre-Beatle songwriting partnerships, Pomus and Shuman also wrote hits for Dion ('Teenager In Love'), The Drifters ('Save The Last Dance For Me'), and The Searchers ('Sweets For My Sweet'). And in the course of his career, Elvis recorded no fewer than twenty songs written by the pair, including 'A Mess O' Blues', 'Surrender' and 'Viva Las Vegas'. 'Turn Me Loose' was also written specifically for Elvis, but was hijacked and diluted by Fabian.

Pomus and Shuman also contributed the scorching B-side to 'His Latest Flame'. 'Little Sister' was a pounding R&B rocker, for which Elvis growled menacingly. The song resurfaced in 1979, when it was covered by Ry Cooder and Led Zeppelin's Robert Plant.

The double-sided assault of 'Little Sister' and 'His Latest Flame' delighted the longer-standing Elvis fans. Liberated at last from the cloying constraints of his recent big ballad offerings, here was a rare reminder of the early Presley, the one who had rocked and rolled his way through the 50s. But it was to be a short-lived liberation. The King's next No.1 would be a ballad again – one of the biggest sellers of his career and a song with which he would remain inextricably linked until the end of his life.

The A–Z of Elvis

Q is for Queer Elvis

In the vast pantheon of Elvis impersonators at large in the late 20th century, few came as close to capturing the feminine side of the King as Elvis Herselvis who performed with her band, The Straight White Males. Madonna may well have remarked of k.d. lang that, 'Elvis is alive, and she's beautiful', but that just goes to show that Madge had never seen Elvis Herselvis. Formerly Leigh Crow of San Francisco, Elvis Herselvis began her career miming to Elvis songs in Drag King clubs (Drag Kings are women dressed as men) in the SF Bay area in 1990. Over the next ten years she built a huge following on the Gay and Drag King circuit of the US playing and singing Elvis songs. In 2001, Elvis Herselvis submerged her professional talents into a cross-dressing supergroup with fellow Drag Kings Jen Gandy and Deena Davenport. They rocked the house at the 6th International Drag King Contest later that year. Elvis himself, of course, was purely heterosexual, even if he did tend to have a somewhat homoerotic effect upon otherwise straight men in the 50s – and beyond, as the Christian Slater character in the Quentin Tarantino-penned, Oliver Stone-produced and Tony Scott-directed movie *True Romance* (1993) points out. Twice. See also the entry for 'Jailhouse Rock'.

CAN'T HELP FALLING IN LOVE

Written by George David Weiss, Hugo Peretti, Luigi Creatore

Recorded 23 March 1961 at Radio Recorders Studios, Hollywood

Guitar: Scotty Moore, Hank Garland, Tiny Timbrell
Bass: Bob Moore
Drums: D.J. Fontana, Hal Blaine, Bernie Mattinson
Piano: Floyd Cramer
Saxophone: Boots Randolph
Harmonica: George Fields
Ukelele: Fred Tavares, Alvin Rey
Vocals: The Jordanaires, The Surfers

Released 21 November 1961

With the benefit of hindsight, films like *Blue Hawaii* can be seen as successive nails in the coffin of Elvis Presley's reputation, but back when they were first released in 1961, there was no denying their bright, colourful, confident charm.

In Britain, where Elvis was destined never to appear in concert, there were still only two television channels, both in black and white; popular music on the radio was strictly rationed by the BBC; and there was not yet any press coverage of pop idols outside of the weekly, inky music press. No videos. No internet. No CDs or DVDs or MTV ... Truly the dark ages.

Three times a year though, parched Presley fans would be drip-fed bright, big-screen confectionery like *Blue Hawaii*. The synopsis says it all: 'Chad Gates (Elvis) is back in Honolulu after his discharge from the army trying to figure out what to do with his life. One thing he knows for sure is that it won't be joining the family pineapple business ... ' But in 1961 *Blue Hawaii* was apparently just what cinema-going audiences wanted for an undemanding Saturday night treat.

It was what Scotty Moore characterised as one of the 'rubber stamp movies'. But though critics may carp, *Blue Hawaii* went on to become the most successful of all of Elvis' films. And its success gave the Colonel all the more reason to push Elvis further and further along the route of vapid, brightly

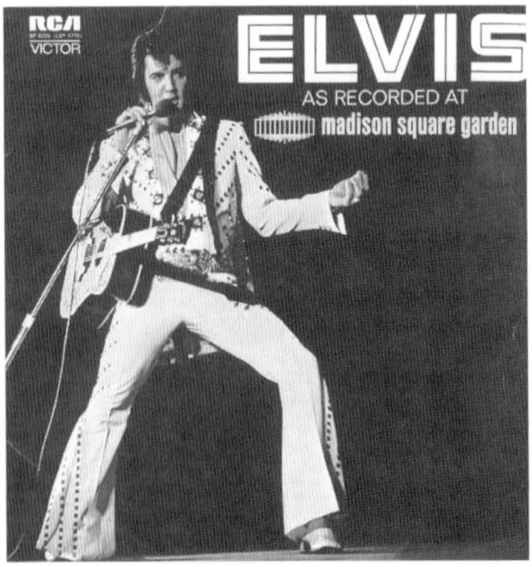

The LP sleeve of the Madison Square Garden recording that features one of Elvis' greatest performances of 'Can't Help Falling In Love'.

coloured travelogues – each offering increasingly diminishing returns.

Much to the delight of Colonel Parker, the success of the film itself was reflected in the sales of the soundtrack album: *Blue Hawaii* remained at No.1 on the American album charts for an astonishing twenty weeks, the longest run of any Elvis LP. Even today, *Blue Hawaii* still holds the record as the biggest-selling Elvis soundtrack album of all time – and much of that success was down to just one song.

When 'Can't Help Falling In Love' is first heard in the film it is playing on a music-box; of course, Elvis soon takes over, but that truncated music-box version from the movie can still be heard on the expanded 1997 CD of *Blue Hawaii*.

Like 'It's Now Or Never' and 'Surrender', 'Can't Help Falling In Love' was based on a much older song, in this case, the classical 18th-century French 'Plaisir d'Amour'. It was undeniably an enchanting melody – Joan Baez faithfully recorded the original, as did The Seekers, Nana Mouskouri and Marianne Faithfull. But with new lyrics specifically written for him, 'Can't Help Falling In Love' went on to become synonymous with Elvis and when he returned to the concert stage during the 70s, he would use 'Can't Help Falling In Love' as his final encore.

The song went on to become a Top 5 hit for Andy Williams and The Stylistics in the 70s, but no matter how often the song is covered, 'Can't Help Falling

'I LOVE THE ELVIS MOVIES. I USED TO WATCH THEM. IN EVERY SINGLE ONE OF HIS MOVIES HE WASN'T ACTING AS A CAR SALESMAN – HE WAS ACTING AS A CAR SALESMAN WHO LOVED TO PLAY THE GUITAR'

Larry Mullen, U2

Can't Help Falling in Love

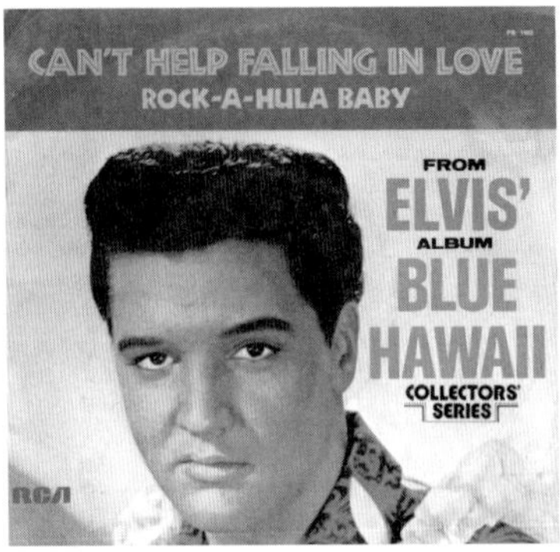

In Love' will remain forever linked with Elvis Presley. The track displays Elvis' rich, velvety voice to perfection. Its insistent, stately melody weaves across the song, while Elvis injects the lyrics with a sincerity he rarely matched on disc. There is something devotional, almost inspirational, about the song – and particularly the singer's performance of it. The lustrous pitch of Elvis' voice caresses the words right from the all-knowing opening line. (Although it was actually Alexander Pope who first said 'fools rush in…', making him the second classic English writer to be quoted on an Elvis Presley single, after Shakespeare.)

'Can't Help Falling In Love' is taken at a leisurely and unhurried pace, yet Elvis manages to infuse it with a real sense of drama and purpose. He is reflective, but full of questions; besotted, yet unsure of the future. One thing that is certain though, is his sincerity. He is not just, in the words of Johnny Ace – another of Elvis' favourite singers – 'Pledging My Love'; here Elvis is pledging his life.

The song is unquestionably one of Elvis' greatest performances as a balladeer and an instructive example of his consummate mastery of how to perform a popular song. The way Elvis handled 'Can't Help Falling In Love' proved once and for all that he had a way with a song that few beside Sinatra could equal. 'Can't Help Falling In Love' is perhaps the definitive example of Elvis Presley as song interpreter – technically sublime, but also managing to connect emotionally, it demonstrated the King's true genius.

French sleeve artwork for an 80s re-release of 'Can't Help Falling In Love'.

Long-time Elvis fan Bruce Springsteen made a point of performing 'Can't Help Falling In Love' (and a re-written 'Follow That Dream') extensively during his triumphant 1981 European tour; a few years later Lick The Tins inventively reworked 'Can't Help Falling In Love' as a joyous Irish lament; and in 1993 the song reached No.1 again in the UK in a version by UB40.

U2's Bono lived out his Elvis fantasy when he sang 'Can't Help Falling In Love' on the soundtrack of *Honeymoon In Vegas* – a film unique inasmuch as it also featured a plane-load of sky-diving Elvis impersonators at its climax. (See Elvis A-Z, F is for Flying Elvi.) In 1970, even Bob Dylan crooned his way through 'Can't Help Falling In Love'. The song truly did seem to have taken on a life of its own. But it remains, indelibly and inextricably, Elvis' song.

The A–Z of Elvis

R is for Reality

Something that Elvis was never in touch with too much. As he sang in 'Edge Of Reality', recorded in March 1968 for inclusion in possibly the weirdest movie he made, *Live A Little, Love A Little*, 'Here's where life's dream lies disillusioned, the edge of reality'. Although it was recorded just as he was making his big comeback, the downward spiral of drug over-consumption had begun and the Vegas-time life where day becomes night and vice versa, was about to begin in earnest. For most of his life, Elvis had been protected from the harsher realities of existence. Firstly by his beloved mother, then by Red West at school, by the Memphis Mafia at Graceland and on tour and finally by barbituates, uppers, downers and various painkillers administered by his team of doctors led by Dr Nick – George Nichopoulos. To Elvis, reality was being able to fly to Washington unannounced and get in to see the President of the United States without an appointment. Reality to Elvis was wearing a cape and spangly jumpsuit and shooting off guns in the backyard whenever he pleased. Reality to Elvis was ordering a deep-fried peanut butter and banana sub sandwich whenever he wanted one and eating it in bed. Perhaps most importantly however, Elvis' reality was not being around to save his beloved mother from dying of, as he saw it, a broken heart. When he entered the Army it marked the longest and furthest distance from her that he'd ever been. For a man who'd slept in the same bed as his momma until his early teens, that was a cruel reality.

GOOD LUCK CHARM

Written by Aaron Schroeder and Wally Gold

Recorded 25 October 1961 at RCA Studios, Nashville

Guitar: Scotty Moore, Jerry Kennedy
Bass: Bob Moore
Drums: D.J. Fontana, Buddy Harman
Piano: Floyd Cramer
Saxophone: Boots Randolph
Vocals: The Jordanaires

Released 27 February 1962

While 'Good Luck Charm' may not feature on many fans' lists of all-time favourites, it did give Elvis his first No.1 of 1962. In America, the song was his sixteenth No.1, but it would also prove to be his last American chart-topper until 1969.

In Britain, however, his fortunes were still on the rise. 'Good Luck Charm' gave Elvis his eleventh No.1 hit and set him on his way to breaking yet another record: 'Good Luck Charm' reached No.1 in May 1962, and was followed to the top by every single Elvis released in the UK that year, meaning that he reigned at the top of the chart for fifteen out of 52 weeks during 1962. Added to his successes the previous year, this meant Elvis had achieved an incredible total of 33 weeks in the No.1 slot over the previous two years – a record which has never, and will never, be beaten.

'Good Luck Charm' was co-written by Aaron Schroeder, giving him his fourth No.1 with Elvis, following 'Big Hunk O' Love', 'Stuck On You' and 'It's Now Or Never'. An undemanding mid-paced rocker, 'Good Luck Charm' did have a certain charm but, even in 1962, it already sounded a little bit dated. It was as if Elvis, who had led from the front for so long, was beginning to find the effort of it all too much. In truth, 'Good Luck Charm' could just as easily have been a hit for Bobby Vee, or Frankie Avalon, or Tommy Sands, or Fabian ...

With its infectious 'uh-huh-huh' backing from The Jordanaires, and loping bass from Bob Moore, 'Good Luck Charm' eases along nicely enough, but it is hard to escape the fact that this was little more than quintessential early 60s' easy listening music – indeed, the once edgy and confrontational Elvis here sounds like he could be singing in a cardigan.

Both 'Good Luck Charm' and its B-side, the poignant Don Robertson ballad 'Anything That's Part Of You', were recorded at Elvis' final non-film session of 1961. Studio sessions now had to be

Good Luck Charm

From the 1968 NBC Television comeback special.

squeezed in between film commitments, and time pressures meant that Elvis very rarely took more than half a dozen takes, max, to record anything.

'Good Luck Charm' rose effortlessly to No.1 – but then the competition wasn't stiff. In Britain, skiffle had come and gone; trad jazz was on the wane; Chubby Checker, Sam Cooke and even Frank Sinatra had got in on the Twist phenomenon; and heads were scratched over the impenetrable lyrics of Karl Denver's 'Wimoweh'. Instrumentally, Acker Bilk and Kenny Ball ruled, while TV themes from *Dr Kildare*, *Z Cars* and *Maigret* helped pad out the charts. With 'Good Luck Charm' occupying the top slot, it was all very safe, and cosy, as if the 50s hadn't quite fizzled out – but waiting in the wings, the 60s were about to kick off with a vengeance.

In New York Bob Dylan had begun recording his second album, *The Freewheelin' Bob Dylan*, which contained the landmark anthem 'Blowin' In The Wind'. Basements in Hamburg and Liverpool already pulsated to the bracing new beat of The Beatles. And on 6 June 1962, with 'Good Luck Charm' still at No.1, The Beatles auditioned for EMI at their Abbey Road studios.

'I PICKED UP THE GUITAR BECAUSE I WANTED TO BE LIKE ELVIS PRESLEY'

Paul Simon

SHE'S NOT YOU

Written by Doc Pomus, Mike Stoller, Jerry Leiber

Recorded: 19 March 1962 at RCA Studios, Nashville

Guitar: Scotty Moore, Harold Bradley, Grady Martin
Bass: Bob Moore
Drums: D.J. Fontana, Buddy Harman
Piano: Floyd Cramer
Saxophone: Boots Randolph
Vocals: The Jordanaires

Released 17 July 1962

She's Not You

The Elvis bandwagon seemed unstoppable: 'She's Not You' was released as Elvis began filming *Girls! Girls! Girls!*. The idea had been for Elvis to record a new album rather than a film soundtrack and to that end, the ubiquitous Freddy Bienstock was asked to trawl through the song catalogues for suitable material. The result was *Pot Luck* – a real potpourri, as its name suggested, and incredibly, Elvis' first non-soundtrack album for five years.

By 1962, Elvis and the Colonel were working to a well-worn formula. Elvis found the film work undemanding and any outside considerations were handled by the Colonel, who negotiated top-dollar deals for all the films and in turn reaped the benefits of the soundtrack albums. The film sold the album and the albums got fans in to see the films. There was really no *need* to record separate singles and albums when the movie soundtracks were already out there in the marketplace. Besides, the Colonel had the songwriting side all sewn up: why venture outside the Hill & Range, Elvis Presley and Gladys Music catalogues? Okay, the calibre of the songs might leave something to be desired, but they certainly helped boost the cashflow for the Colonel and his client.

'She's Not You' was a rare collaboration between Doc Pomus, Jerry Leiber and Mike Stoller – a country-flavoured song, written to order for the *Pot Luck* album. Given its songwriting pedigree, perhaps a little more might have been anticipated, but at least the single did

An original UK single pressing of 'She's Not You'.

the job that was expected of it, by continuing Elvis' seemingly endless run of hits.

Boots Randolph's sax lurks just by your right ear, and in the tradition of all those soft, safe, mid-paced Presley rockers, the Jordanaires ooh-woo for all they're worth in the background, while Elvis coasts through his vocal lead. There is little real drama in the song, but there's just enough undemanding melodrama to satisfy the tastes of the period.

The B-side of 'She's Not You', the pacy 'Just Tell Her Jim Said Hello', bore the familiar Leiber and Stoller credit, and is cut in a similar relaxed groove. But the session also produced another strong Doc Pomus and Mort Shuman song, the Latin-flavoured 'Suspicion'. Although the song was inexplicably consigned to a Presley B-side, Terry Stafford would earn his fifteen minutes of fame when he took 'Suspicion' to the charts in early 1964.

With his film roles and songs such as 'She's Not You' and 'Good Luck Charm' Elvis was fast establishing himself as the king of lounge. Like the European dynasties in the summer of 1914, Elvis had no reason to suspect that life would not continue with him crooning and churning out films. But in the world outside, the fans were chafing – there was some great pop music around, why wasn't Elvis, of all people, making it?

The A–Z of Elvis

S is for Songwriter

Like Frank Sinatra before him, and unlike anyone else in rock music after, Elvis was a major singing superstar who generally didn't write his own songs. Although, again like Sinatra, when it came to the most important woman in his life Elvis did put pen to paper. Sinatra co-wrote 'I'm A Fool To Want You' when he was grieving over his break-up with Ava Gardner. Elvis co-wrote 'That's Someone You'll Never Forget' with his best friend Red West after the death of Gladys. He, Red and fellow Memphis Mafia founder Charlie Hodge also wrote 'You'll Be Gone', a song of praise for the one-night stand. While there may be some doubt as to the actual size of his contribution, at least Elvis was in the room when they were being written. Which can't be said for the rest of the numbers with which he's co-credited. There were seven such numbers, including most of the hits that Otis Blackwell came up with for him (see entry for 'Don't Be Cruel'). This despite the fact that Elvis never met Otis. Elvis is also credited with co-writing four songs with Vera Matson, including 'Love Me Tender' (see entry), for his first movie in 1956. There is also a credit for writing the latter half of the 'I Got My Mojo Working/Keep Your Hands Off Of It' track recorded in May 1970, most of which sounds like an improvisation on Muddy Waters' original song. As well as co-writing, Elvis is credited with arranging and adapting a whole host of the spirituals and Christmas carols that he recorded.

RETURN TO SENDER

Written by Otis Blackwell, Winfield Scott

Recorded 26 February 1962 at Radio Recorders, Hollywood

Guitar: Scotty Moore, Barney Kessel, Tiny Timbrell
Bass: Ray Siegal
Drums: D.J. Fontana, Hal Blaine, Bernie Mattinson
Piano: Dudley Brooks
Saxophone: Boots Randolph
Vocals: The Jordanaires

Released 2 October 1962

Return To Sender

Even die-hard Elvis fans were hard-pushed to find anything particularly memorable about his eleventh film, *Girls! Girls! Girls!* – the movie's one redeeming feature was a song that was never intended for the soundtrack, but that would briefly rejuvenate Elvis' musical career. Released as a single before the film opened, 'Return To Sender' sold over two million copies and remained in the American Top 40 for fourteen weeks.

A welcome addition to the Presley canon, 'Return To Sender' also proved to be a watershed. It would be another seven years before Elvis enjoyed a No.1 again in his homeland and he would never spend that long on the US chart with any of his subsequent single releases.

'Return To Sender' came courtesy of Otis Blackwell, who had already provided a brace of No.1s for Elvis with 'Don't Be Cruel' and 'All Shook Up' – helped out this time around by Winfield Scott, who had written LaVern Baker's 'Tweedle Dee'. But there was an energy in the song that came directly from Elvis – an energy which had been noticeably absent from much of his recent soundtrack work. Elvis would run through his film songs willingly enough, but his heart and mind were plainly elsewhere. As a result of the deals the Colonel was cutting with songwriters during the early 60s, Elvis realised that he was no longer getting the best material, but he could still recognise a good song when he was lucky enough to hear one – and 'Return To Sender' was one of the best he had heard for a long time.

Introduced by a honking sax, there is a jaunty immediacy to the song – a deftly told tale of a letter that can never be delivered to the singer's true love – and Elvis carried the song beautifully. British listeners were a little baffled, in those pre-post code days, by the 'zones' referred to in the lyric, but they still went out and bought it in droves, giving Elvis that year's Christmas No.1. In America, with overall

Elvis entertains co-stars of *Girls! Girls! Girls!* 1962.

sales in excess of two million, 'Return To Sender' gave Elvis his third platinum disc of the year.

The rest of the tracks on the *Girls! Girls! Girls!* soundtrack didn't exactly set fans' hearts fluttering – aside from the rocking 'Return To Sender', the album included such fishy fillers as 'Song Of The Shrimps'. Yet such was the momentum of the Presley juggernaut, that even this tawdry soundtrack became a Top 3 album on both sides of the Atlantic.

'Return To Sender' came back into vogue in 1993 when, on the day that would have been his 58th birthday, the US Post Office issued an Elvis Presley stamp. It was too good an opportunity to miss and many fans deliberately mis-addressed their first-day issues so that they would get them back – marked 'Return To Sender'.

'I WASN'T EXACTLY JAMES BOND IN *DOUBLE TROUBLE*, BUT THEN, NO ONE EVER ASKED SEAN CONNERY TO SING A SONG WHILE DODGING BULLETS'

Elvis Presley

(YOU'RE THE) DEVIL IN DISGUISE

Written by Bill Giant, Bernie Baum, Florence Kaye

Recorded 26 May 1963 at RCA Studios, Nashville

Guitar: Scotty Moore, Harold Bradley, Grady Martin, Jerry Kennedy
Bass: Bob Moore
Drums: D.J. Fontana, Buddy Harman
Piano: Floyd Cramer
Saxophone: Boots Randolph
Vocals: The Jordanaires

Released 28 June 1963

Devil In Desguise

The song may have been written by committee, but it was a formula that paid off. '(You're The) Devil In Disguise' was without doubt one of Elvis' more energetic singles of the early 60s: the opening, shuffling Bo Diddley beat is immediately overtaken by Bob Moore's bass, sounding as thick and lustrous as a hot fudge sundae. There's a guitar hovering somewhere off to the side; the percussion is inventive; and the overall melody pounds along like a Harley on a dirt road.

Given that the entire song runs to less than two-and-a-half minutes, there are an astonishing number of tempo changes. Lyrically too, the song is more inventive than most recent Presley hits of the time. The idea of the object of affection being a devil is imaginatively sustained, and for the first time in a long time, Elvis sounds like he's having as much fun as his fans.

No-one would compare its impact to that of the ground-breaking 'Heartbreak Hotel', but at least with 'Devil In Disguise' Presley once again displayed his command of the pure pop single. But it was to prove a short-lived triumph, the very success of '(You're The) Devil In Disguise' indicating the end of an era for Elvis.

The record's desultory predecessor, the undistinguished 94-second 'One Broken Heart For Sale', had already set alarm bells ringing at RCA some months before. 'One Broken Heart For Sale' was the first single by Elvis Presley to stall outside the American and British Top 10 in five years. Taken from the soundtrack of the 1963 vehicle, *It Happened At The World's Fair,* even hardcore Elvis fans felt they had been short-changed this time, with an entire soundtrack album that ran for barely twenty minutes.

Hard to credit after seven extraordinary and unparalleled years at the top, but by the summer of

Elvis in costume for *Roustabout*, 1964.

The so-called 'Lost Album', *For The Asking* featuring 'Devil In Disguise'.

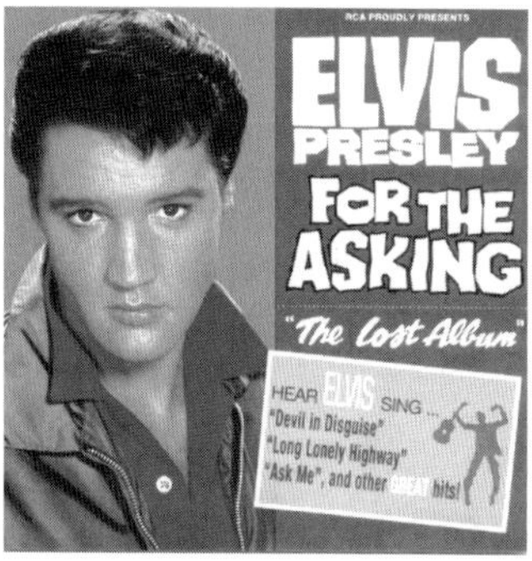

1963, almost overnight, Elvis Presley had become an anachronism. By the time Elvis reached No.1 in the UK with 'Devil In Disguise', British fans were grappling with a new word in the teenage dictionary – 'Beatlemania!' Elvis' fluffy, insubstantial and now embarrassingly old-fashioned films were particularly at odds with the vivacious new music and groovy public image of The Beatles and Rolling Stones. There was a natural wit and immediacy to The Beatles from early on, and that spontaneity was sadly absent from the glossy celluloid image of Elvis.

Unknown to Elvis – and indeed the music industry as a whole – the real threat posed by The Beatles was that of their own masterly songwriting team. Not for them that tedious sift through the uninspired song catalogues of tried and tested songwriters writing to a formula. Thanks to Lennon and McCartney – as well as the inspired production techniques of George Martin – a new Beatles single could come at you from almost anywhere.

For the first time since he shot to fame in 1956, Elvis faced stiff, serious and sustained competition. The Beatles' arrival in America in February 1964 was a mere foretaste of the Beatlemania that would follow: the high-water mark of the group's American invasion came on 4 April 1964. That was the week when The Beatles were at No.1 with 'Can't Buy Me Love' – which had racked up unprecedented advance sales of over two million copies – but they also held all four of the remaining places in that week's Top 5 *and* a further seven entries on the Hot 100. (The following week, though they lost their monopoly of the hallowed Top 5, two new chart entries gave The Beatles a total of fourteen Hot 100 hits at one time.)

In achieving this chart Olympus, The Beatles shattered the record previously held by Elvis, who in 1956 had managed nine singles on the charts simultaneously. That same year, the King had enjoyed two consecutive No.1 singles – but that record too was taken from him when The Beatles' 'She Loves You' replaced 'I Want To Hold Your Hand' at No.1 – only to be deposed in turn by 'Can't Buy Me Love'.

To make matters worse, it soon became clear that this was only the beginning. In the wake of The Beatles came the Stones, and The Searchers, The Animals, The Kinks, The Who, Billy J. Kramer, The Dave Clark 5, Manfred Mann ... The British Invasion was underway.

When '(You're The) Devil In Disguise' reached No.1 in Britain during August 1963, The Beatles were still little more than an engaging English phenomenon. Like their predecessors Lonnie Donegan, Acker Bilk and The Tornados, there was little to indicate that they could sustain any real American success. But at home, that success was now a done-deal.

It is to Elvis' credit then, that between 3 January 1963 and 25 June 1964, 77 whole weeks, he was the only American act to reach No.1 on the British singles charts, with '(You're The) Devil In Disguise'. It was quite an achievement, but the writing was clearly on the wall.

'HE TAUGHT WHITE AMERICA TO GET DOWN'

James Brown

The A–Z of Elvis

T is for Tupelo

The birthplace of Elvis. The two-room shack, built by Vernon for $180, now stands as The Elvis Presley Museum and the road in which it stands has been re-named Elvis Presley Drive. The museum contains various articles of Presley memorabilia including a pair of Elvis' biker boots and a jumpsuit. Other Presley-related locations of interest include the Assembly of God Church on Adams Street where Gladys and Elvis used to attend services; Lawhon and Milam Junior High schools which Elvis attended until the eighth grade and his move to Memphis; the Tupelo Hardware store where Elvis' first guitar was bought and the Tupelo Fairgrounds at which the King performed two triumphant homecoming concerts in 1956 and 1957. There is also an Elvis Presley Lake and Campground covering 850 acres and offering a range of boating and camping activities all year round. Being rightly proud of its association with Elvis, Tupelo arranges several Elvis-related events each year in the name of the king of rock'n'roll. In 2002 there was an Elvis Presley festival on 31 May and 1 June, Riding With The King bicycle races on 6 June and, although not held in the name of Elvis, surely something of which he would heartily approve – the Tupelo Gigantic Flea Market–Knife and Gun Show in midsummer.

CRYING IN THE CHAPEL

Written by Artie Glenn

Recorded 30 October 1960 at RCA Studios, Nashville

Guitar: Scotty Moore, Hank Garland, Elvis Presley
Bass: Bob Moore
Drums: D.J. Fontana, Buddy Harman
Piano: Floyd Cramer
Saxophone: Boots Randolph
Vocals: The Jordanaires

Released 6 April 1965

Crying In The Chapel

There was never any doubting that gospel had played a formative part in the life and music of Elvis Presley. Growing up in Memphis, gospel music was all around him; and for the rest of his life, throughout that extraordinary arc which took him to the top of the world, Elvis maintained a fondness for the power and the glory of the music that echoed around the churches of his youth.

Early on, Elvis had discovered the solace to be drawn from gospel music and, as a teenager, he regularly attended all-night gospel meetings at Memphis' Ellis Auditorium, standing out amongst the predominantly black crowd. And later, when the world went mad and Elvis was at the epicentre, he always warmed up in the studio with the gospel material he knew so intimately – songs recorded by The Blackwood Brothers, The Statesman Quartet and The Trumpeters.

Whether recording in Nashville, or relaxing at home in Bad Nauheim or Graceland, gospel music was always close at hand. And remember, when The Million Dollar Quartet of Elvis, Jerry Lee Lewis, Johnny Cash and Carl Perkins convened spontaneously at Sun Records on 4 December 1956, it wasn't the rock'n'rollers who won out.

Just a glance at the songs played at that session gives a good idea of where Elvis' heart lay – 'Just A Little Walk With Jesus', 'Blessed Jesus Hold My Hand', 'Peace In The Valley', 'Down By The Riverside', 'I Shall Not Be Moved' ... A dozen years on and his tastes hadn't changed: one of the highlights of Elvis' 1968 comeback TV special was a gospel segment featuring the voice of the magnificent Darlene Love, with Elvis confidently reasserting his roots.

There was no denying the intensity of Elvis' gospel performances, on record or on stage. He may have whipped up a wave of sexual frenzy in America in 1956, but Elvis was also the courteous Southern boy who still addressed every stranger as 'Sir' or

'Ma'am'. Elvis Presley was no saint, but he never forgot where he drew his inspiration from – and the church remained his foundation.

That battle of the saviour in the right hand and the devil in the left raged long and hard in the souls of many a southern-bred rock'n'roller. They believed sincerely that at the last trumpet sinners would roast in the fires of perdition, but on the other hand, the lure of earthly pleasures was strong. Perhaps that tension was best and most vividly illustrated in an incident that occurred at Sun Studios, as Jerry Lee Lewis struggled against Sam Phillips, apparently in the belief that he was fighting for his very soul.

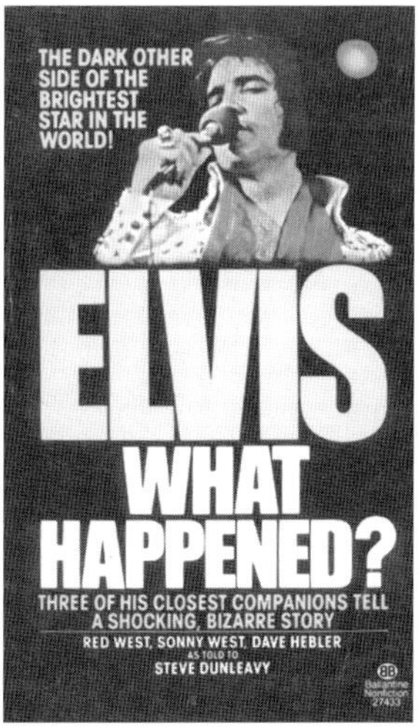

The cover of the book that broke Elvis' heart: *Elvis What Happened?* by Red and Sonny West andDave Hebler.

It is the summer of 1957 and Jerry Lee is about to cut 'Great Balls Of Fire', a song written for him by Otis Blackwell. The tension is palpable: somehow the fiery pianist has become convinced that rock'n'roll is, quite literally, the devil's music. Sam Phillips, with one eye on the studio clock, tries desperately to convince him otherwise. 'I've got the devil in me,' Jerry Lee roars at one point. It was the eternal conflict for poor white boys from the Bible Belt like Jerry Lee, like Elvis.

'PEOPLE LIKE MYSELF, MICK JAGGER AND ALL THE OTHERS ONLY REALLY FOLLOWED IN HIS FOOTSTEPS'

Rod Stewart

'Crying In The Chapel' came from the all-night session six months after his army demob, at which Elvis recorded his No.1 single, 'Surrender', as well as the twelve songs that made up the album *His Hand In Mine*. As early as 1957, while he was still a sultry rock'n'roller scandalising the nation, Elvis had released an EP of inspirational material called *Peace*

In The Valley; but *His Hand In Mine*, which was released in time for Christmas 1960, was the first time Elvis had released an entire album of devotional songs.

Although recorded in 1960, 'Crying In The Chapel' didn't make it onto *His Hand In Mine*, instead appearing seven years later on Elvis' second album of inspirational material, *How Great Thou Art*.

'If you're looking for trouble . . .' Elvis in action, NBC-TV Special, 1968.

All Elvis' gospel recordings were later gathered together on the 1994 double CD *Amazing Grace – The Greatest Sacred Performances*. It is worth remembering that in his entire career Elvis only ever won three Grammy Awards, and all three were for his gospel recordings.

Elvis remembered 'Crying In The Chapel' from a 1953 recording by Sonny Til & The Orioles – and, as ever when Elvis sang religious material, there was no doubting the sincerity he brought to his performance. There is certainly an added lustre to Elvis' singing on 'Crying In The Chapel', as if he himself was part of a congregation, gathered together to praise the Lord in a place where he could still find contentment, happiness and peace of mind. It seemed he could lose himself more completely in gospel music than in any other, letting the rhythm wash over him and immersing himself totally in the familiar lyrics.

Incredibly, 'Crying In The Chapel' reached No.1 in the British charts in June 1965. That was the year when The Beatles effortlessly upped the ante on pop music with their *Rubber Soul* album; the year Bob Dylan broke through on to the charts; and when The Rolling Stones' songwriting fluency finally began to match that of Lennon and McCartney. Elvis was only 30 at the time, but the King of rock'n'roll now found himself competing against newcomers like Sonny &

Cher, The Byrds, Donovan, The Who, Manfred Mann, Joan Baez, Tom Jones, Gene Pitney and The Animals. For other reasons too, the success of 'Crying In The Chapel' was particularly satisfying for Elvis: the fact that it was his first British No.1 in two years; his first American million-seller since 'Devil In Disguise'; his first major hit since the breakthrough of The Beatles – and all this with a spiritual song, a song with a message.

For much of the 60s, Elvis was consumed by a quest for spiritual enlightenment: obsessed with finding out what his purpose on earth was; why the Lord had singled him out; why he had survived when his twin brother had died; why his beloved mother had been taken from him so early; what lay ahead after this life on earth. And by the middle of the decade, when 'Crying In The Chapel' became a hit, that quest had already swung off into eastern religions, spiritualism, philosophy. But at the time he recorded the song all that lay in the future, and the devotion you can hear in Elvis' performance reflects the strong and simple religious roots of his childhood.

It was to be a long time before Elvis Presley made any real impact on the charts again, either in Britain or America – and it would be a further four years before his next No.1. By then, the world of rock'n'roll would have undergone its most seismic changes since Elvis had first burst upon the scene back in 1956.

The A–Z of Elvis

U is for Undead

Nobody wanted to believe that Elvis had died. There are many people who still refuse to believe it. Two thousand years ago Elvis would have been the figurehead of a new religion (but then again, two thousand years ago there weren't any burger bars, supermarket checkouts or gas stations at which to spot him, so maybe not). Because so many of the unpleasant details of Elvis' death were kept secret immediately following his demise, it was natural that conspiracy theories about his disappearance would grow. The most commonly held belief about Elvis' 'faked death' is that he did it so that he could live a normal life without interruption. There have been books published purporting to tell the truth about his disappearance and non-death (one came with a cassette tape of a post-death telephone conversation) and numerous tabloid-reported sightings. There's a long-running website on which people can post their experiences of spotting Elvis – http://www.elvissightingbulletinboard.com. A personal favourite sighting is dated 29 March 2001 and claims that Elvis has converted to Judaism and is living quietly in Israel having become enlightened by David. The posting asks us to respect his privacy. Yet, as sad as it may be, the fact remains that Elvis is dead. Although not completely gone, of course, as the many hundreds of thousands of people who pay to watch the Virtual Elvis Tours will happily testify.

IN THE GHETTO

Written by Mac Davis

Recorded 20 January 1969 at American Sound Studios, Memphis

Guitar: Reggie Young
Bass: Tommy Cogbill, Mike Leech
Drums: Gene Chrisman
Piano: Bobby Wood
Organ: Bobby Emmons
Steel Guitar: John Hughey
Harmonica: Ed Kollis
Horns: The Memphis Horns
Vocals: Mary Green, Mary Holladay, Donna Thatcher, Susan Pilkington, Sandy Posey

Released 14 April 1969

In The Ghetto

Not surprisingly, the success of 'Crying In The Chapel' – which had, after all, been recorded five years before – proved to be a one-off. Throughout the remainder of the 60s, you could *feel* the torpor setting in, as Elvis resigned himself to simply going through the motion-picture motions. In October 1963, *Kissin' Cousins* was shot in seventeen days, and when the studio realised they could take their star and turn out a film that quickly, it gave a whole new meaning to the word 'exploitation'.

Elvis' career was suffering anyway in the wake of Beatlemania – his May 1964 release, 'Kiss Me Quick', was the worst-selling single of his career. Now, while The Beatles, The Beach Boys and Bob Dylan competed with each other to expand the horizons of popular music, the man who had started it all was stuck in Hollywood churning out forgettable film fluff like *Fun In Acapulco, Viva Las Vegas* and *Tickle Me.*

Inevitably, the inferiority of the films was reflected in the songs recorded for the soundtracks. It became increasingly hard to reconcile the rebel who had rocked the world with 'Heartbreak Hotel', 'All Shook Up' and 'Rip It Up' with the Hollywood star offering us 'Thanks To The Rolling Sea', 'Do The Clam', 'No Room To Rhumba In A Sports Car' and 'Fort Lauderdale Chamber Of Commerce'.

In January 1965, a symbolic event occurred on the American charts when a cobbled-together Beatles album (*Beatles '65*) knocked an Elvis Presley album (*Roustabout*) off the top of the charts for the first time. Later that year, Elvis Presley and The Beatles met. It was 27 August 1965, and group and singer were both equally nervous.

The meeting was hardly the rock'n'roll summit you might anticipate. Instead while Colonel Parker and Brian Epstein sat off to one side discussing business matters, the Fab Four made inconsequential small-talk with the King. Paul McCartney and Ringo Starr found the remote-control that enabled Elvis to

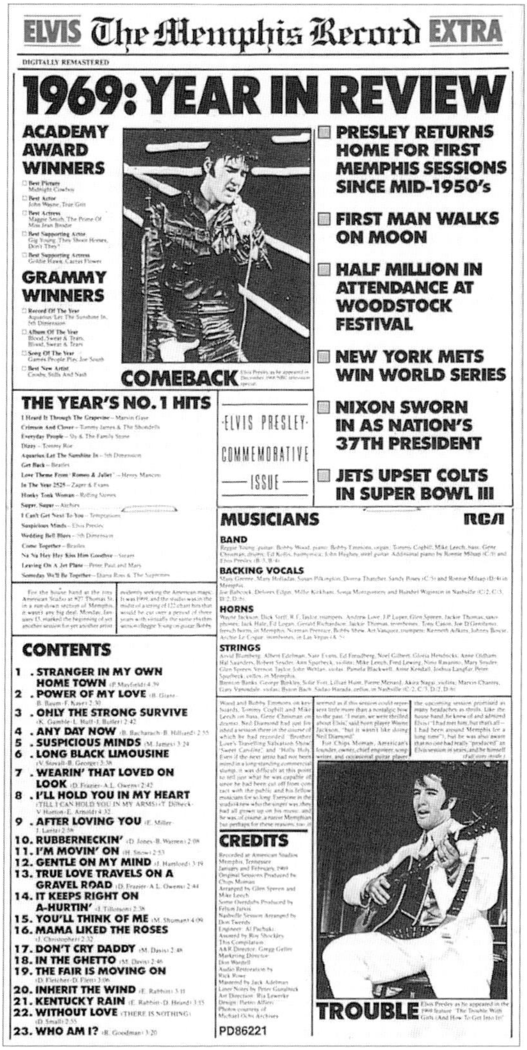
ELVIS The Memphis Record EXTRA

DIGITALLY REMASTERED

1969: YEAR IN REVIEW

ACADEMY AWARD WINNERS

- Best Picture
  Midnight Cowboy
- Best Actor
  John Wayne, True Grit
- Best Actress
  Maggie Smith, The Prime Of Miss Jean Brodie
- Best Supporting Actor
  Gig Young, They Shoot Horses, Don't They?
- Best Supporting Actress
  Goldie Hawn, Cactus Flower

GRAMMY WINNERS

- Record Of The Year
  Aquarius/Let The Sunshine In, 5th Dimension
- Album Of The Year
  Blood, Sweat & Tears, Blood, Sweat & Tears
- Song Of The Year
  Games People Play, Joe South
- Best New Artist
  Crosby, Stills And Nash

COMEBACK

- PRESLEY RETURNS HOME FOR FIRST MEMPHIS SESSIONS SINCE MID-1950's
- FIRST MAN WALKS ON MOON
- HALF MILLION IN ATTENDANCE AT WOODSTOCK FESTIVAL
- NEW YORK METS WIN WORLD SERIES
- NIXON SWORN IN AS NATION'S 37TH PRESIDENT
- JETS UPSET COLTS IN SUPER BOWL III

THE YEAR'S NO. 1 HITS

I Heard It Through The Grapevine – Marvin Gaye
Crimson And Clover – Tommy James & The Shondells
Everyday People – Sly & The Family Stone
Dizzy – Tommy Roe
Aquarius/Let The Sunshine In – 5th Dimension
Get Back – Beatles
Love Theme From "Romeo & Juliet" – Henry Mancini
In The Year 2525 – Zager & Evans
Honky Tonk Woman – Rolling Stones
Sugar, Sugar – Archies
I Can't Get Next To You – Temptations
Suspicious Minds – Elvis Presley
Wedding Bell Blues – 5th Dimension
Come Together – Beatles
Na Na Hey Hey Kiss Him Goodbye – Steam
Leaving On A Jet Plane – Peter, Paul and Mary
Someday We'll Be Together – Diana Ross & The Supremes

·ELVIS PRESLEY·
COMMEMORATIVE
— ISSUE —

MUSICIANS

RCA

BAND

BACKING VOCALS

HORNS

STRINGS

CONTENTS

1. STRANGER IN MY OWN HOME TOWN (P. Mayfield) 4:39
2. POWER OF MY LOVE (B. Giant-B. Baum-F. Kaye) 2:30
3. ONLY THE STRONG SURVIVE (K. Gamble-L. Huff-J. Butler) 2:42
4. ANY DAY NOW (B. Bacharach-B. Hilliard) 2:55
5. SUSPICIOUS MINDS (M. James) 3:24
6. LONG BLACK LIMOUSINE (V. Stovall-B. George) 3:38
7. WEARIN' THAT LOVED ON LOOK (D. Frazier-A.L. Owens) 2:42
8. I'LL HOLD YOU IN MY HEART (TILL I CAN HOLD YOU IN MY ARMS) (T. Dilbeck-V. Horton-E. Arnold) 4:32
9. AFTER LOVING YOU (E. Miller-J. Lantz) 2:56
10. RUBBERNECKIN' (D. Jones-B. Warren) 2:08
11. I'M MOVIN' ON (H. Snow) 2:53
12. GENTLE ON MY MIND (J. Hartford) 3:19
13. TRUE LOVE TRAVELS ON A GRAVEL ROAD (D. Frazier-A.L. Owens) 2:44
14. IT KEEPS RIGHT ON A-HURTIN' (J. Tillotson) 2:38
15. YOU'LL THINK OF ME (M. Shuman) 4:09
16. MAMA LIKED THE ROSES (J. Christopher) 2:32
17. DON'T CRY DADDY (M. Davis) 2:48
18. IN THE GHETTO (M. Davis) 2:46
19. THE FAIR IS MOVING ON (D. Fletcher-D. Flett) 3:06
20. INHERIT THE WIND (E. Rabbitt) 3:11
21. KENTUCKY RAIN (E. Rabbitt-D. Heard) 3:15
22. WITHOUT LOVE (THERE IS NOTHING) (D. Small) 2:55
23. WHO AM I? (R. Goodman) 3:20

CREDITS

PD86221

TROUBLE

Arguably the greatest album Elvis ever made. All songs recorded in Memphis in early 1969.

change TV channels without leaving his sofa at least as fascinating as anything their idol had to say. John Lennon later went on record to say how disappointing it had been, but at the time he was virtually speechless at being in his presence.

Midway through the 60s, with audiences in their millions turning on to The Beatles, Elvis began to be seen as a relic from another era. His songs and films

'THERE HAVE BEEN MANY ACCOLADES UTTERED ABOUT HIS TALENT AND PERFORMANCES THROUGH THE YEARS ALL OF WHICH I AGREE WITH WHOLEHEARTEDLY. I SHALL MISS HIM DEARLY AS A FRIEND' Frank Sinatra

were increasingly out of step with the changing times – it was a time of Carnaby Street and James Bond, 'Like A Rolling Stone' and 'Yesterday'; not Graceland and 'Yoga Is As Yoga Does'.

While Elvis clunked dutifully through soundtrack recordings for *Harum Scarum* and *Paradise, Hawaiian Style*, outside, the walls were shaking. Here, Bob Dylan and The Beatles, both of whom had initially been inspired by Elvis, were rewriting the rock'n'roll rulebook with albums like *Revolver* and *Highway 61 Revisited*. They were creating their own worlds of 'Eleanor Rigby' and 'Desolation Row' while Elvis was left churning out three forgettable films a year.

Just occasionally, amidst all the weary songs submitted for his film soundtracks, Elvis would find something that touched him. And perhaps surprisingly, despite all the dross he had to perform, his musical tastes were still immaculate. During 1965 he even went through a bit of a folk jag, listening to albums by Peter, Paul & Mary and Odetta at Graceland. The *Odetta Sings Dylan* album led Elvis to cover an obscure Dylan original ('Tomorrow Is A Long Time'), which later found an incongruous setting on the soundtrack of *Spinout!* Asked in 1969 if he had a particular favourite out of all the cover versions that had been recorded of his own songs, Dylan replied that the one he treasured most was Elvis' cover of 'Tomorrow Is A Long Time'.

Elvis had recorded the Dylan song at a May 1966 session, which marked the first time in three years he had returned to RCA's Nashville Studios for a full, non-soundtrack session. As well as the Dylan cover, it produced a version of 'Love Letters', originally a hit for Dick Haymes in 1945, which took Elvis to No.6 in Britain. But throughout 1966, and for the next two years, not one of Elvis' releases would crack the Top 10 in America.

By 1967, we find Elvis filming *Clambake*, while The Beatles are busy recording *Sgt Pepper*. As Elvis commences filming *Speedway*, Jimi Hendrix and The Who electrify Monterey at the world's first rock festival; and while Elvis' *Easy Come, Easy Go* came and went, The Doors, Pink Floyd, Velvet Underground, and Procol Harum all released ground-breaking debut albums.

1967 will forever be remembered as the Summer of Love. 'Love children' were seen all over the streets of San Francisco – the city where you had to wear flowers in your hair. And all over the world, the soundtrack of that year was provided by the epochal *Sgt Pepper*, Procol Harum's haunting 'A Whiter Shade Of Pale' and The Beatles' anthemic 'All You Need Is Love'. In Britain, the establishment was concerned by the hippies' increasing reliance on drugs and a warning shot was fired across the bows when the Rolling Stones were busted for drug offences.

The A–Z of Elvis

V is for Vernon Presley

There is a widely held belief among psychologists that the disappearance of Vernon from Elvis' life when the King was three (Vernon was jailed for passing bad cheques) had a profound effect upon Elvis' emotional development. At that age a child naturally goes through a separation anxiety from its mother, which fathers can often help with. Elvis only had Gladys. They slept in the same bed up until Elvis was a young teen. Elvis loved his father, of course. But a big part of that love was probably based upon his mother's love for the elder Presley. After the death of Gladys, Elvis kept Vernon close and welcomed his father's second family into his own home (Vernon's second wife Dee had three young sons, all of whom moved into Graceland). Vernon loved his son but hated his Mafia. It was he who fired the Wests and Hebler in 1976, prompting their penning of *Elvis: What Happened?*. Vernon would usually tour with Elvis, making very occasional appearances on stage with the King. The last time he did so was at the end of the last stop on the final Elvis live tour of 1977, on stage at the Market Square Arena in front of 18,000 fans on 26 June. In what was to be the last photograph of the men together, the elder Presley is in much better physical shape than the younger. His stomach is smaller, as is the buckle on the belt of his white flared trousers. The buckle on Elvis' waistband serves to highlight the bulge above it. Two years to the day later, Vernon died of a heart attack in Memphis.

It was a time of convulsive social change everywhere, a year when the old morality and established values were threatened. But 1967 was also the year that the original anti-establishment figure, Elvis Presley, chose to get married. Elvis had first become acquainted with Priscilla Beaulieu eight years previously, while he was serving with the Army in Germany. When he met the dark-haired beauty, the step-daughter of a serving US Army captain, she was only fourteen years old – but from the outset, Elvis was captivated.

On his departure from Germany, a picture of the tearful Priscilla had appeared in *Life* magazine above the caption: 'Girl He Left Behind'. But the relationship continued at long distance, until in 1963 Priscilla came to live with Elvis at Graceland. Priscilla was a striking companion for Elvis – petite and with her perfect face framed by jet-black hair, she had the same serene beauty as the young Elizabeth Taylor. On 1 May 1967, in Las Vegas, 32-year-old Elvis Presley wed his young bride. Nine months later, the couple's only child, Lisa Marie would be born.

Behind the walls of Graceland, marriage and imminent fatherhood made Elvis a happy man as 1968 began. Professionally though, his life looked set to carry on the same lucrative but unfulfilling course. Elvis seemed to have resigned himself to being locked away in Hollywood studios, making dreary and repetitive movies and music that he plainly no longer believed in. Until, mid-way through 1968, Elvis finally realised that he *had* to do something to escape this remorseless three-movies-a-year treadmill.

The Colonel had long been touting the idea of a Christmas special, to be aired on American television in December 1968. The emphasis was heavily on Christmas and Elvis imagined himself standing there, running through the same festive songs he had first recorded a decade earlier. It was only after meeting the TV executives, all of whom were zealous in their desire to get the galvanising,

One of the defining Elvis images: in action at the beginning of the NBCV-TV Special, 1968 in a black leather suit.

Elvis and Priscilla marry in Las Vegas, 1967. They were separated in 1972.

mesmerising Elvis of old back onto their screens, that Elvis began to have second thoughts.

Like the rest of America, Elvis had been shocked by the murder of Martin Luther King in Memphis that summer, and the assassination of Robert Kennedy in August had only compounded his grief. Those tragedies helped reinforce director Steve Binder's vision that Elvis' TV special should be used as an opportunity for the singer to *say* something, rather than simply wrapping up the year on a cheesy Christmas note. Elvis agreed wholeheartedly.

The Colonel was still pushing for a Christmas single, but Elvis was now confident enough to start tugging in another direction. Jerry Reed's 'Guitar Man' and 'US Male' had given him a couple of hits earlier in the year and his fans had been delighted by their infectious, rootsy feel. And so it was that the Colonel's 1968 Christmas special became something no one could have imagined: the most remarkable comeback in the history of rock'n'roll.

Squeezed into a black leather jumpsuit, his sideburns back to their pre-army length, a tanned and slimmed-down Elvis returned to claim his crown. All manner of scenarios were considered for the special – and all were rejected, until Steve Binder managed to convince Elvis simply to rely on his musical instincts. One of the show's greatest treats was the sight of Elvis jamming once again with his favourite musicians. Guitarist Scotty Moore and drummer D.J. Fontana were back on board for the first time in a decade, as Elvis reminisced.

Here was Elvis made flesh once more: mocking his celluloid image, remembering the controversy his suggestive stage movements had created back in 1956. Above all, here was Elvis electrifying again, with energetic reworkings of his biggest hits – 'Heartbreak Hotel', 'Jailhouse Rock', 'All Shook Up', 'Can't Help Falling In Love' – all sung in front of an audience who couldn't quite believe their luck.

On screen it all seemed so natural. But this was his first television appearance since the Sinatra comeback special nearly a decade before, and backstage before filming began Elvis was paralysed with fear. He kept threatening to withdraw, terrified that he'd dry up on camera. But despite his nerves about facing a live audience for the first time in years, Elvis returned to his musical roots in triumph.

At the climax of the show, instead of the Colonel's original choice of 'I'll Be Home For Christmas', Elvis concluded with Earl Brown's specially written 'If I Can Dream'. It was a song that captured the 60s' optimism, but at the same time reflected on the harsher realities of 1968 – a year tarnished by war, riot and assassination.

Energised by the success of his TV special, Elvis was finally ready to get recording seriously again – and early in 1969, he returned to Memphis, to undertake his first sessions there in fourteen years.

'HE'S A GREAT SINGER. GOSH, HE'S SO GREAT. YOU HAVE NO IDEA HOW GREAT HE REALLY IS, REALLY YOU DON'T'

Phil Spector

This was the first time since leaving Sam Phillips' Sun Records that Elvis was back in a Memphis recording studio. Recording at American Sound Studios carried a real cachet: Dusty Springfield had cut her classic *Dusty In Memphis* album there, and the studio had also played host to Wilson Pickett, Dionne Warwick and The Box Tops.

'HE COMPLETELY CHANGED THE WAY I FELT ABOUT MUSIC. HE COMBINED EVERYTHING THAT A STAR NEEDS. LOOKS, CHARISMA, TALENT AND ORIGINALITY'

Elton John

In The Ghetto

Elvis arrived at American on 13 January 1969, fresh from the success of the TV special and with 'If I Can Dream' riding high in the charts, but he was as nervous about the forthcoming ten-day session as he had been about his recent television appearance.

For the first time in the decade, Elvis had escaped from Hollywood and RCA's Nashville studios. American Sound's players were experienced session-men who were not in awe of Elvis. His nervousness was apparent and he was experiencing vocal problems – some of the session musicians voiced their disappointment that Neil Diamond had been forced to cancel to make way for Elvis. But in the event, Elvis got into a groove during that first ten-day burst, and those 1969 recording sessions at American Sound now rank alongside the seminal Sun sessions and pivotal RCA Nashville recordings.

It wasn't just the studio or the musicians, or the euphoria at having escaped from his recent rut. Elvis was really getting off on the new music – songs by young songwriters like Mac Davis, Mark James and Eddie Rabbitt were striking a real chord with him. And after years of being numbed by mediocrity, Elvis was finally getting back in touch with his instincts.

Thanks to the songs of Bob Dylan and the work of Simon and Garfunkel, Joan Baez and Peter, Paul & Mary, 'protest' music was already an integral part of the music scene by early 1969. Elvis had even tried out Dylan's 'Blowin' In The Wind' at home, but in the end decided to restrict his protests to complaining to Colonel Parker about the quality of the material he was expected to sing.

As a teenager in 1955, Mac Davis had seen Elvis play his home town of Lubbock, but by the time Elvis came to record his material, Mac had already written hits for Lou Rawls, O.C. Smith and Kenny Rogers. Elvis' recording of Mac Davis' 'In The Ghetto' would, however, transform both their lives.

'In The Ghetto' was the song that really brought Elvis back into play. He obviously responded to the song's sentiments and the American Sound musicians locked on to the beat from early on, but Elvis cared enough about this song to spend 23 takes getting it just right.

The song's original title, 'The Vicious Circle', was thought too strong for Elvis; but while the title may have been softened, the strength of his performance on the finished song was evident. America had been riven by violent confrontation throughout the 60s: race riots had torn apart Los Angeles and anti-Vietnam demonstrations raged nationwide. But 'In The Ghetto' wasn't a call to arms, rather a gentle reflection in the vein of Dylan's 'Blowin' In The Wind' or Sam Cooke's 'A Change Is Gonna Come'.

When 'In The Ghetto' was released in Britain, Elvis found himself competing with the Rolling Stones at their most lascivious ('Honky Tonk Women') and John Lennon at his most militant ('Give Peace A Chance'), but still he managed to replace Thunderclap Newman's 'Something In the Air' at No.1 in the *NME* chart. In America the record only reached No.3 while The Beatles' 'Get Back' enjoyed a five-week residency at No.1.

From the very first take, Elvis' singing on 'In The Ghetto' was as fine as at any time in his career. The song develops and builds – bass and guitar pick out the melody; the drums are staccato and military; while the backing vocals offer call and response to the pleading vocal, sounding eerie and otherworldly, affecting in a way that the comforting 'doo-doo' accompaniment of The Jordanaires would never be again. But in the end the song is carried by the heroic vocal, with Presley injecting drama, pain, passion and hope in a way that nobody else could.

SUSPICIOUS MINDS

Written by Mark James

Recorded 22 January 1969 at American Sound Studios, Memphis

Guitar: Reggie Young
Bass: Tommy Cogbill, Mike Leech
Drums: Gene Chrisman
Piano: Bobby Wood
Organ: Bobby Emmons
Steel Guitar: John Hughey
Harmonica: Ed Kollis
Horns: The Memphis Horns
Vocals: Mary Green, Mary Holladay, Donna Thatcher, Susan Pilkington, Sandy Posey

Released 26 August 1969

Following the success of 'In The Ghetto', Elvis vowed that he would never sing another song he didn't believe in. Sadly, the vow was broken all too soon, but in the immediate aftermath came 'Suspicious Minds' – a song that many regard not just as his greatest single of the 60s, but arguably the greatest-ever Elvis recording.

Elvis was always a great interpretive singer, and nowhere is his dramatic ability better demonstrated than on 'Suspicious Minds'. He was obviously energised by his stint at American Sound and, significantly, 'Suspicious Minds' was the last track to be recorded at that first ten-day session. He did return a fortnight later for another five-day burst, which produced the great 'Kentucky Rain' – but beyond any doubt, the true highlight of those early 1969 sessions remains 'Suspicious Minds'.

Recognising the greatness of the song instinctively, Elvis nailed it in four takes, not leaving the studio until 7am. 'Suspicious Minds' had come from American Sounds' resident songwriter Mark James, a Houston native who wrote two other Elvis hits, 'Always On My Mind' and 'It's Only Love'. He also wrote 'Hooked On A Feeling', which was a British hit for Jonathan King. James had recorded 'Suspicious Minds' himself in 1968 and producer Chips Moman returned to the powerful backing of that version when Elvis came to cut the song early the following year.

Right from the nagging opening guitar figure, 'Suspicious Minds' sounds like a potentially great single. As soon as Elvis comes in, that greatness is confirmed. This is a song of moods and dramatic changes. The orchestration and backing vocals are lush; the drums and guitar lend a neurotic edge; Elvis sounds fragile and vulnerable. 'Suspicious Minds' combines all the high drama of grand opera with the simple visceral appeal of pop music – brought together in a peerless Presley performance.

Elvis in white jumpsuit gives it all, his way, circa 1973.

At nearly four and a half minutes, 'Suspicious Minds' is almost twice as long as many of his previous hit singles. But not a note is wasted, and the false ending is a stroke of genius: Elvis is still caught in that trap, as the song fades, then swells magnificently with his return. It is a triumphant coda, and a magnificent return to form.

This is an adult record, a song about love betrayed and trust replaced by suspicion. At a time when rock'n'roll was flexing itself, with extended drum solos and guitar virtuosi, the discipline of 'Suspicious Minds' was all the more impressive. The fact that this was Elvis, back from the brink, made it doubly so. For those who are only familiar with 'Suspicious Minds' from videos of Elvis in overblown white suits, using the song as little more than a springboard for on-stage karate moves, it is rewarding to return to the original version and marvel as it builds and swells, dives and falls, epic in both intention and execution.

'Suspicious Minds' was the song Chips Moman had most wanted Elvis to try out when he came to American Sound to record in January 1969. His belief was repaid when, in November 1969, 'Suspicious Minds' gave Elvis Presley his first American No.1 for seven long years and his last of the decade. It really was a considerable achievement given that the climate had changed so dramatically during the intervening years. Perhaps the best example of the seismic shifts that had overtaken pop music was that while Elvis was busy planning his return to the concert stage at a lavish hotel in Las Vegas, a completely different type of live event was being prepared in upstate New York.

The legendary Woodstock festival, which began on 15 August 1969, wasn't actually held in Woodstock. The festival site was located at Bethel, some 60 miles from Woodstock, but Bob Dylan lived in Woodstock so Woodstock it became. In the event, Dylan didn't make it to Woodstock. And nor did Elvis. But more than half a million people were drawn to that muddy field for three days of peace, music and love. Woodstock marked the high watermark of the hippie movement – barely a month before the festival, man had first walked upon the moon, and as the dazed survivors trudged wearily home it really did seem as though anything was now possible.

A month before the release of 'Suspicious Minds' and just a fortnight before Woodstock, Elvis Presley finally returned to the concert stage after a gap of eight years. But as he waited in the wings of the International Hotel on 31 July 1969, the nerves that had preceded his appearance on the previous year's TV special were back again, and worse than ever. In March 1961 – the last time he had appeared in concert before a paying audience – Eisenhower was in the White House and Macmillan was still Prime Minister. Young British teenagers like The Beatles and the fledgling Rolling Stones were still unsigned and playing local clubs, waiting for their big break, while in the charts, the King continued to reign supreme.

'I REMEMBER WHEN I WAS NINE YEARS OLD AND I WAS SITTIN' IN FRONT OF THE TV SET AND MY MOTHER HAD ED SULLIVAN ON, AND ON CAME ELVIS. I REMEMBER RIGHT FROM THAT TIME, I LOOKED AT HER AND SAID, "I WANNA BE JUST LIKE THAT"'

Bruce Springsteen

Fast forward to 1969, and the world had turned upside down. America was split over the far-away war in Vietnam; recreational drugs were openly used; and in the cinemas, the frothy escapism of Elvis' films had been superseded by such clarion calls of the counter-culture as *The Graduate* and *Easy Rider*.

On record, Pink Floyd, The Nice, Jimi Hendrix and King Crimson were taking rock to hitherto unimagined heights. The Beatles, unable to replicate the increasingly complex sounds they were fashioning in the studio, had already withdrawn from live performance; but as the 60s drew to a close, bands like Cream, Santana, Led Zeppelin and The Grateful Dead were all out there pushing back the boundaries of concert performance.

It was a dazzlingly different backdrop against which Elvis now displayed himself. The sands had shifted, and though the shows were eagerly awaited, Elvis was plainly nervous. He had spent long weeks selecting and rehearsing the hand-picked musicians who were to accompany him during those crucial comeback shows. The band was led by master-guitarist James Burton, who Elvis remembered from his work with Ricky Nelson during the 50s; while one of the Sweet Inspirations, Elvis' backing group in Las Vegas, was none other than Cissy Houston, mother of Whitney.

At Elvis' invitation, Sam Phillips was amongst those seated in the audience at the International Hotel. Few other performers could have mustered an opening night crowd that included film legend Cary Grant as well as protest singer Phil Ochs. The two-thousand-strong crowd gave him a standing ovation before he even sang a note, which took some of the edge off Elvis' nerves, and from then on in it was a triumph.

With a nod to those early days at Sun, the show opened with Carl Perkins' 'Blue Suede Shoes', before moving on to the first number Elvis had ever cut for RCA, way back in 1956 – Ray Charles' 'I Got A Woman'. 'All Shook Up' did just that, while 'Love Me Tender' cooled the temperature down, only for it to soar again during a powerful medley of 'Jailhouse Rock' and 'Don't Be Cruel'.

It was so much more than anyone could have expected after all those years away from the spotlight, and the reviews were ecstatic. Across the board, from the conservative mainstream press to 'underground' magazines like *Rolling Stone,* the critics as well as the public were unanimous. The

Live, 1970.

creative rebirth heralded by the month-long Las Vegas residency was soon confirmed by the chart success of 'Suspicious Minds', and once again, it really did seem as though Elvis was back at the top of his game.

But few among the crowds who saw the shows that summer, or flocked to buy the single, could possibly have guessed that the King's superb triumph would be so short-lived.

The A–Z of Elvis

W is for Welsh Connections

The Welsh have had a bad press for the last few decades. Ridiculed for inventing the eisteddfod, their historical reliance upon sheep farming and their insistence on speaking an ancient, indecipherable language, the Welsh have had nothing to be proud of since Tom Jones left the Welsh Valleys for the California Valley back in the 60s. Welsh soccer is a joke and any new, young music performer is forced into performing a duet with Tom Jones before they can be accepted as having 'made it'. Therefore it should have come as a welcome surprise when Raeto West 'discovered' Elvis Presley's Welsh ancestry in 1998. Mr West found a 5,000-year-old burial ground in Dyfed wherein lay the remains of St Elvis Cromlech, St Elvis having been St David's (the patron saint of Wales) religious teacher. Mr West also noted that nearby were the Preseli hills, from where the stones of Stonehenge are rumoured to be hewn. Add to this Mr West's suggestion that Jesse Garon could have been a derivative of Geraint, a common Welsh name of the 20th century, and you have good grounds for claiming Elvis' descent from Welsh ancestors.

The enterprising Mr West e-mailed the Welsh tourist authority to suggest that they play up his Elvis connection theory, for which he'd accept a measly 1% of turnover from increased tourism. They replied that they weren't interested. Just wait Raeto. They will be. Never forget how much Elvis liked watching Tom Jones in action in Vegas.

THE WONDER OF YOU

Written by Baker Knight

Recorded 18 February 1970 at The International Hotel, Las Vegas

Guitar: James Burton, John Wilkinson, Charlie Hodge
Bass: Jerry Scheff
Drums: Bob Lanning
Piano: Glen Hardin
Vocals: The Imperials, The Sweet Inspirations
Featuring Bobby Morris & His Orchestra

Released 20 April 1970

Originally recorded by Ray Petersen in 1959, 'The Wonder Of You' was the first live recording Elvis had ever issued as a single – ironically, it also gave him the last British No.1 he would live to see.

The recording came from Elvis' second series of concerts at the International Hotel, Las Vegas, which began on 26 January 1970. Buoyed by the reception given to his shows the previous summer, Elvis returned to the gambling capital in triumphant mood. He had been energised by his return to the concert stage and the subsequent success of 'Suspicious Minds'; and, much to his relief, Elvis had at last worked out his contractual obligations in Hollywood – *The Trouble With Girls* and *Change Of Habit*, both released during 1969, effectively brought the curtain down on Elvis Presley's celluloid career.

The Las Vegas shows could only add lustre to the Elvis legend – and for once he had the stage pretty much to himself. Bob Dylan was about to ease himself out of the public eye for three years. The Beatles, preoccupied with dragging their sorry split through the law courts, were now out of the frame. And the Rolling Stones, still recovering from their Altamont festival the previous December, at which a fan had been murdered by Hell's Angels, were preparing to go into tax exile in the South of France.

'ELVIS IS MY MAN'

Janis Joplin

'The Wonder Of You' was a gloriously overblown ballad of the kind Elvis came increasingly to favour during his years in Vegas. As ever though, his singing is spot-on and the instrumental backing, perfect.

Pianist Glen Hardin – a native of Lubbock, Texas, who had played with Buddy Holly's Crickets – was responsible for the sumptuous arrangements, which

undoubtedly played their part in the record's success. The vaudeville brass opening is soon swamped by a lush orchestra; Elvis' vocal entrance is fresh and confident; and the orchestration emphasises the vocal histrionics perfectly, lending a real sense of awe and drama to the song.

Elvis in jumpsuit and rhinestones, 1973.

'The Wonder Of You' acts as a forcible reminder that while easing himself into the 70s, Elvis wasn't content merely to coast on former glories. By now, he was completely at ease with his backing band – 'Play it Jimmy,' Elvis gently instructs, as James Burton undertakes a muted solo. And as the number concludes on a dramatic note, it becomes apparent that his singing voice had been enriched by the twice-nightly performances.

On 15 August 1970, 'The Wonder Of You' took Elvis to the top of the British charts. Again, he had faced strong competition. The Elvis' single sprinted past such classics as The Kinks' 'Lola', Smokey Robinson's 'Tears Of A Clown' and Free's 'All Right Now', and once established at No.1, it remained there for six weeks.

The odd picture sleeve for the US release of 'The Wonder Of You'. Who is that in the picture?

Elvis was also making a good show in the album charts. The live album of his Vegas shows, *On Stage: February 1970*, held up well against *Let it Be, Bridge Over Troubled Water, Led Zeppelin II*, Dylan's *Self-Portrait, McCartney* and *Deep Purple In Rock*. Elvis was once again finding favour, thanks in part to his recordings of songs by contemporary acts like The Beatles and Creedence Clearwater Revival.

Hopes were high for the future. Free at last from the Hollywood film factory, Elvis' spell at the International Hotel had confirmed his return to live performance – and triumphantly so. Surely, fans reasoned, this meant Elvis would perform regularly from now on; that he might even tour – perhaps after all these years, fans in Britain, France, Germany, Italy and Spain would finally be rewarded for their loyalty. But, as it turned out, Elvis never did get to Europe – or, indeed, anywhere else outside of North America.

While the legendary Las Vegas comeback had been widely reported, few of Elvis' devoted fans around the world had actually seen the shows. The currency restrictions applied by the UK government in the late 60s made it particularly difficult for British fans to make the pilgrimage to Las Vegas; although in 1972, at an all-inclusive cost of £175 each for fourteen days, 193 fans from The Official Elvis Presley Fan Club of Great Britain did finally make it to America to see Elvis perform.

Those who witnessed Elvis in performance during 1969 and 1970 may have been ecstatic, but they were a tiny minority of his worldwide constituency. Most fans outside America had to be content with another film. But those with nagging memories of *Tickle Me* or *Harum Scarum* were in for a surprise – this was a very different sort of Elvis film.

The cover of one of the best live Elvis releases.

Released in November 1970, the film *Elvis: That's The Way It Is* was a triumph. As the booklet that accompanied the soundtrack's thirtieth-anniversary release n oted: 'RCA recorded while MGM filmed, over the course of four consecutive nights, capturing an incredibly lean, charismatic and mischievous Elvis at the height of his vocal powers. For literally millions of Elvis fans around the world, *That's The Way It Is* was a revelation. Expectations were high after the success of the 1968 NBC-TV show but few expected Elvis to return to centre-stage in such a contemporary way after years in the wilderness during the late 60s.'

Within four days of finishing his Vegas shows, Elvis flew to Texas to give three performances at the Annual Texas Livestock Show, which was taking place in the 70,000 capacity Houston Astrodome. Elvis wasn't very happy with the sound at the world's largest venue, but nonetheless netted a cool $1,200,000 for the engagement.

Sadly, the scale of these Houston shows set the seal on his live performances for the remainder of the decade. Free at last from the likes of *Fun In Acapulco*, Elvis seems almost immediately to have replaced one lucrative treadmill with another.

One person who did manage to see the King up close and personal was the President. By now Elvis had metamorphosed into a deeply conservative member of the establishment. Earlier in 1970, America had been convulsed by the murder of four student protesters at Kent State, and massive anti-war demonstrations now clogged city streets throughout the country – and at such a bitter time in the nation's history, the sight of Elvis Presley consorting with the President was anathema to many who had followed him since 1956.

The king of rock'n'roll had come to embody the very values he had challenged during the mid-50s. By the early 70s, law and order had become one of Elvis' main obsessions and the apogee of this obsession came on 21 December 1970, when he got to meet the nation's top cop, US President Richard M. Nixon. The photos of Nixon meeting Elvis have a surreal air. Elvis is in caped crusader costume, and although the President was only halfway through his first term of office and Watergate still lay in the future, the jowly Nixon is easily recognisable as the future hate-figure of the American left.

This strange meeting had been set in motion when Elvis met Senator George Murphy on a flight and gave the conservative politician a letter to pass on to the President. In it, Elvis expressed his concern about the parlous state of America, which he saw as being undermined by hippies, Black Panthers, drugs, students and communists. In his letter, Elvis pleaded to be given federal credentials enabling him to wage a one-man crusade against the enemy.

During the later years of his life, Elvis obsessively collected police and FBI memorabilia and one of his proudest possessions was the Narcotics Bureau badge that President Nixon presented to him after their meeting. Guns too played a part in the increasingly fantastical world Elvis was now living in. Typical was a spending spree at a Memphis gunsmith late in 1970, when Elvis lavished $20,000 on firearms he intended to give as Christmas presents. One famous anecdote from Elvis' later years concerns the King at home in Graceland – incensed by the sight of singer Robert Goulet on television, he took out a gun and blew the set apart.

It was during his 1970 Las Vegas concerts that Elvis began favouring the white jumpsuits that would become a hallmark of his 70s' concert appearances. Costing $400 apiece, they gave him the flexibility to move on stage during his early, energetic performances. But it wasn't until the final show of his seventh Las Vegas residency, in September 1971, that Elvis began sporting a cape. Another feature of the later shows was heard first around this time, when announcer Al Dvorin solemnly intoned, 'Elvis has left the building.' A year later, in November 1972, 115 scarves were ordered from Mr Guy in Las Vegas and their dispersal to loyal fans soon became an integral part of Elvis' stage-show.

Gradually, the various elements that would make up the template for Elvis' later stage appearances fell into place – the jumpsuit and cape; the scarves; the announcement … The final piece of the pattern was eventually added during an engagement in Lake Tahoe, Nevada in the summer of 1971, when Elvis first began using that apocalyptic Richard Strauss piece, 'Also Sprach Zarathustra', as an overture.

The A–Z of Elvis

X is for Elvis X

This is undoubtedly the most difficult letter to fulfil for all compilers of Elvis A–Zs. Mick Farren completely ignored the letter in his witty *Hitchhiker's Guide to Elvis* published in 1994. The enterprising Peter Silverton opted for following up an apocryphal story about Russian bootleggers burning Elvis bootlegs from X-ray plates in his hugely entertaining *Essential Elvis* (1998). I, however, have gone for a band from North Carolina who call themselves Elvis X. Why no one had thought of it before 1997, when they formed, is an amazing fact in itself. After all, any searches on Amazon.com for Elvis records are going to throw up anything that they've released too, right? Well, possibly. If they'd released anything we would know, but they don't seem to have. Comprising Bassist Scott Tuttle (ex-Metropolis), singer/ frontman Scott Tucker (ex-Misplaced Aggression), guitarist Steve Muir (ex-Toxic Popsicle), and experimental percussionist Scotty Irving, they are described by the one review I could find on the WWW as 'effectively build(ing) environments of freight-train 'lectronic sounds & guitar-thunder … LOTS OF HUMOR in here too … I keep thinking I've just heard a cartoon theme, then it's gone … this is intelligent & Dadaistic modern rock.' That was by no less an authority than *Improvijazzation* magazine in 2000.

BURNING LOVE

Written by Dennis Linde

Recorded 28 March 1972 at RCA Studios, Hollywood

Guitar: James Burton, John Wilkinson, Charlie Hodge
Bass: Emory Gordy
Drums: Ronnie Tutt
Piano: Glen Hardin
Vocals: J.D. Sumner & The Stamps

Released 1 August 1972

Burning Love

As with his film obligations in the 60s, Elvis' increasing commitment to live performance during the 70s meant that recording sessions were left to be squeezed into the gaps between concerts. In consequence it is estimated that apart from two 'at-home' sessions at Graceland, Elvis ventured into the recording studio less than a dozen times during the whole of the 70s.

For two years following 'The Wonder Of You', all of Elvis' subsequent singles had failed to crack the American Top 10. It couldn't be blamed on either his performances or the choice of songs – in fact, Elvis' recording of 'American Trilogy' probably ranks among the finest of his career. But the young generation of singer-songwriters such as James Taylor, Neil Young and Carole King, together with soft-rock proponents like Bread and The Carpenters, were now monopolising the charts month after month.

Many of those in the King's inner circle suspected that what Elvis needed to return him to the charts was simply a raw slab of rock'n'roll. But what with his newly acquired Vegas-style sensibilities and growing problems in his marriage, Elvis himself was now more inclined towards songs in the vein of 'Suspicious Minds'.

At the specially convened March 1972 session, Red West's 'Separate Ways' and Kris Kristofferson's bitter-sweet 'For The Good Times' were amongst the material he tried out. But on the second night, in just six takes, they got 'Burning Love'.

Elvis himself evinced little real enthusiasm for 'Burning Love', but his producer Felton Jarvis reckoned that re-forging a bond with rock'n'roll could be just the thing to make Elvis a winner again. The song, which had come Elvis' way from Kristofferson's publisher, had a refreshing up-tempo feel and writer Dennis Linde had already seen the song covered unsuccessfully by singer-songwriter

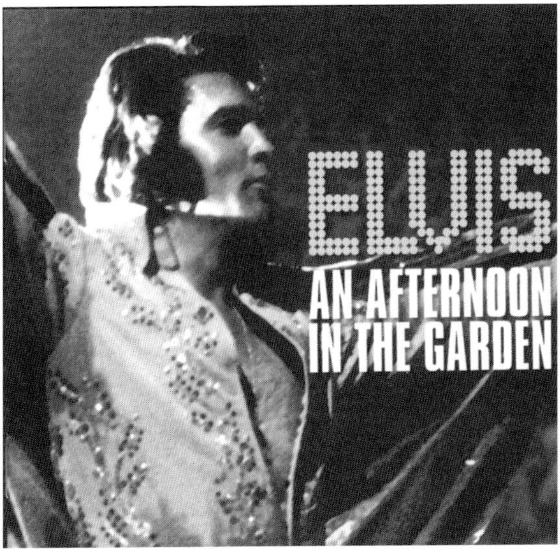

The sleeve for the 1997 release of the recording made of the afternoon performance at Madison Square Garden, June 10, 1972.

Arthur Alexander. Alexander had achieved immortality at a young age: while still in his early twenties he had seen his song 'A Shot Of Rhythm & Blues' become a staple of the early 60s' British beat boom, and later his work would be covered by both The Beatles ('Anna', 'Soldier Of Love') and the Rolling Stones ('You Better Move On').

'Burning Love' was certainly at odds with the type of material Elvis generally favoured during the early 70s. He had found that big ballads went over best with his live audiences – powerhouse performances of songs such as 'Bridge Over Troubled Water', 'The Impossible Dream' (from the film *Man Of La Mancha*) and 'You Don't Have To Say You Love Me' really wowed the crowds and 'Can't Help Falling In Love' was now his regular concert-closer. But even Elvis could see that this style of song cut no ice with the wider record-buying public.

Perhaps because it lacked Elvis' whole-hearted commitment, the finished version of 'Burning Love' sounds thin. If there is a standout performance on the single it is that of drummer Ronnie Tutt, long used to backing Elvis in concert, who powers the song behind the singer. As for Elvis, he may have been back rock and rolling in theory, but he sounds like he was lurking at the far end of the studio when this one was recorded.

On stage, 'Burning Love' did take on the energy and frenzy that Felton Jarvis had always anticipated. But Elvis remained unconvinced and soon dropped it from performance – although ironically, when he did perform the song, the fans lapped it up.

'EVERYONE IN ROCK'N'ROLL INCLUDING MYSELF WAS TOUCHED BY HIS SPIRIT, I WAS, AND ALWAYS WILL BE A FAN'

Bryan Ferry

Burning Love

Out of sight behind the walls of Graceland, while Elvis worked in far-away Hollywood, Priscilla had become accustomed to reading about his extra-marital affairs. He denied them all, but when the press began running statements from Ann-Margaret, his co-star in *Viva Las Vegas,* that she and Elvis were due to be getting married, Priscilla finally put her foot down. Five years later, when her husband returned to live performance and was away in Las Vegas or on tour for weeks, sometimes months, at a time, rumours of his serial infidelities began once again.

The marriage was obviously in trouble, but like the rest of the world, Elvis couldn't really believe that Priscilla didn't want to remain Mrs Presley, whatever the cost. Finally, in July 1972, Priscilla announced her separation from Elvis Presley – ironically, she had fallen in love with Mike Stone, the man Elvis had employed to teach his wife karate.

Elvis and Priscilla were divorced in October 1973, after just six years of marriage. Many close to Elvis cite this as the moment when his sad and irrevocable decline began in earnest.

Between 1970 and 1972, Elvis played nearly 500 live dates. But of them all, perhaps the best remembered was the night Elvis made his concert debut in New York City. Elvis had made his early television appearances live from there; he had recorded at RCA's studios in the city; he had even set sail for Germany from New Jersey; but unbelievably, his show on 9 June 1972 was the first time he had ever performed in New York.

It was a big date for the Big Apple – and in typical record-breaking fashion, Elvis became the first performer ever to sell out four consecutive shows at Madison Square Garden. Even after three years back in front of the spotlight, he was very nervous about his New York debut. Pianist Glen Hardin remembered, in the sleeve notes for the 1997 CD release of *Elvis: An Afternoon In The Garden* (the first time that the 10 June matinee performance had ever been released): 'I'm sure Elvis never sang better than he did at Madison Square Garden. I suppose he thought the fans in the Big Apple might be more demanding, so he turned on the power, and powerful it was!'

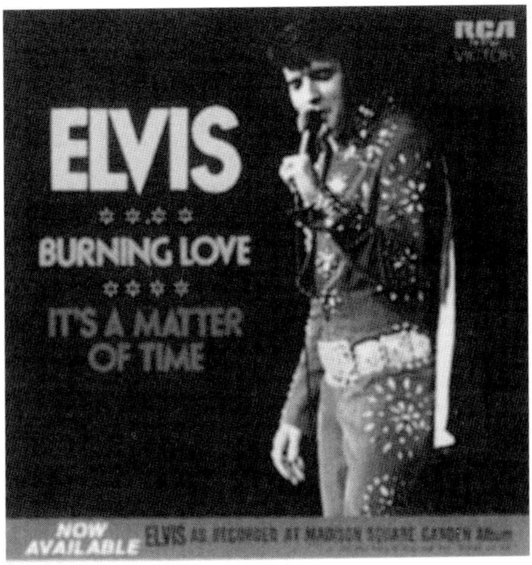

The picture sleeve of the US release of 'Burning Love'.

Playing to audiences of 20,000 at each performance was nerve-wracking enough, but knowing that seated among them were John Lennon, Paul Simon, George Harrison, David Bowie and Bob Dylan can't have eased the Presley nerves. In the event, the shows were critically lauded, and an album, *Elvis, As Recorded At Madison Square Garden,* was released the following week, giving Elvis his most successful album in four years.

With his career now in its third decade, Elvis was once again facing up to some stiff competition. Around the time his Madison Square Garden album

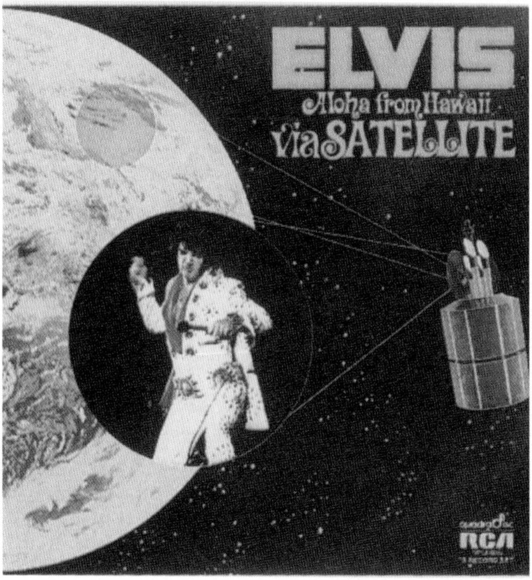

The technology involved that made Elvis' historic live broadcast possible was awesome. As the sleeve for the LP release demonstrates.

Burning Love

charted, he was competing with Paul Simon's solo debut, the Stones' *Exile On Main Street*, Neil Young's *Harvest*, David Bowie's *Ziggy Stardust and The Spiders From Mars*, Cat Stevens' *Teaser & The Firecat*, John Lennon's *Imagine*, Don McLean's *American Pie*, Roxy Music's debut and Lindisfarne's *Fog On The Tyne* – all now regarded as amongst the finest albums of the decade.

Home rehearsals at Graceland reveal Elvis running through an intriguing choice of new material – including two Bob Dylan songs that he never officially recorded (a snatch of 'I Shall Be Released' and a rockabilly take on 'Don't Think Twice It's Alright') which can be found on *Walk A Mile In My Shoes: The Essential 70s Masters* (1995).

The King had reigned fairly effortlessly during the 50s and early 60s, but by the 70s he was struggling to catch the attention of American record buyers: 'Burning Love' was his first million-seller in two years and tragically it would also turn out to be the final US Top 10 hit of his lifetime.

In Britain though it was a very different story, and the scale of Elvis' chart success during the

70s was quite astonishing. Nowadays, Elvis Presley is thought of as being on the margins of what happened during the 70s. Our memories of that time are that the singles charts were ruled by rampaging glam rockers such as Slade, Gary Glitter, Marc Bolan, David Bowie and The Sweet, while the albums charts played host to solo albums by ex-Beatles, and Prog Rockers ELP, Yes, Led Zeppelin and Pink Floyd. But, at the time, it wasn't quite like that.

In the seven years between 1970 and his death, Elvis Presley enjoyed no fewer than twenty Top 20 hits in Britain – including four Top 10 hits in the last year alone. Besides the anniversary reissues, there were such era-defining songs as 'American Trilogy', 'I Just Can't Help Believing', 'Always On My Mind', 'Moody Blue' and the King's energetic reworking of Chuck Berry's 'The Promised Land'.

Meanwhile back at home, as Elvis filled Las Vegas hotel showrooms and 'Burning Love' rode high in the charts, the Colonel was busy plotting. Since Elvis' return to the concert stage in the late 60s, his live appearances had got bigger and bigger – and he was not the only one who believed that bigger was always better. The Rolling Stones, looking for

The A–Z of Elvis

Y is for Yuletide

Elvis loved Christmas. Like all right-minded Christian mommy's boys the world over he'd cry at the holiness, the piety, the sentimentality and the charity of the Yuletide festival. Elvis liked giving presents and didn't need a reason to press a new Cadillac onto the lucky person browsing the lot when he pulled in. He once delivered a pony to the door of a little girl who liked to watch himself and Lisa Marie riding around Memphis. At Christmas Elvis would go extra-gift-giving mad, and it made him feel good. Everyone at Graceland knew that his marriage to Priscilla was more or less over at Christmas 1971 when she asked for $10,000 cash rather than take delivery of yet another new car. Where was the joy for Elvis in that? A year later Elvis presented new girlfriend Linda Thompson with a mink coat. Elvis loved nothing better than dressing the tree, then wrapping and placing presents under it in the wee small hours of 25 December so they'd be ready for Lisa Marie to tear into in the morning. When Lisa Marie stayed with Priscilla for Christmas 1973 the holiday was cancelled. He recorded his first batch of Christmas songs in 1957 and the second in 1971, the recordings of each session being released in numerous variations on two different Elvis Christmas albums, *Elvis Sings The Wonderful World of Christmas* and *Memories of Christmas*. Possibly Elvis' favourite Christmas song – by dint of the fact that it had the word blue in the title – was 'Blue Christmas' which was a hit in 1964 and again in 1965, even though he recorded it in 1957. The same song may well also have provided English glam rock band Mud with the inspiration for their No.1 UK hit single in 1974, 'Lonely This Christmas'.

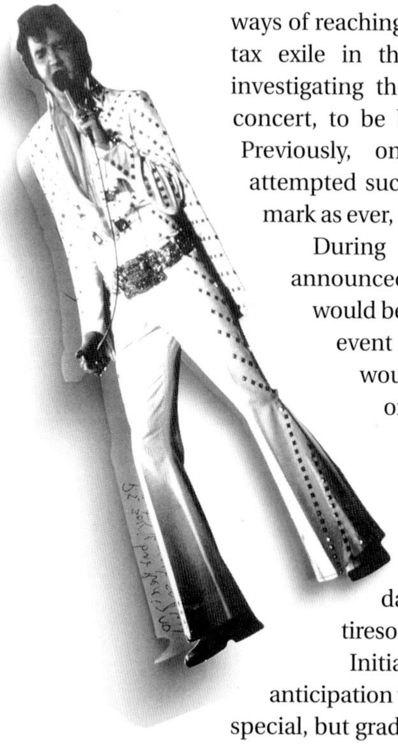

Made in Woodstock, USA, of recycled card, this classic 1970s pose is a consistent best-seller.

ways of reaching their fans while they remained in tax exile in the South of France, had begun investigating the possibilities of a closed-circuit concert, to be broadcast in cinemas worldwide. Previously, only boxing matches had ever attempted such a global link. But, quick off the mark as ever, the Colonel got in there first.

During September 1972, plans were announced for an Elvis television special: it would be the first worldwide entertainment event to be beamed by satellite, and would reach an estimated audience of one billion people. But despite all the record-breaking potential, at the press conference to announce the event Elvis looked bored and jaded. It seemed as though performing too was in danger of become just another tiresome obligation to him.

Initially, there was none of the nervous anticipation that had preceded 1968's comeback special, but gradually, as the true scale of the event dawned on him, Elvis began throwing himself wholeheartedly into the preparations. He took a red pencil to his current stage-set, and began rehearsing a raft of new material. He went on a rigorous diet to lose weight, and by the time he arrived in Hawaii on 9 January 1973, he felt ready to take on the world.

Elvis had just turned 38 when he took to the stage of the Honolulu International Center Arena and the Hawaii satellite show was, arguably, the last genuinely creative challenge of his life. But the event – later released as the cumbersomely titled *Elvis: Aloha From Hawaii Via Satellite* – was another glittering triumph.

The show was watched by a billion people around the world – more than had watched the first moon landing. But the fact that it was shown in 40 countries across the globe was of little comfort to British fans, who felt very short-changed when both the BBC and ITA declined to screen it. They did get the album though – the sixth live Elvis album in four years. But even that glut of live releases didn't stop *Elvis: Aloha From Hawaii Via Satellite* reaching No.1 on the American album charts. It was his first No.1 album in eight years, though sadly it would be the last to achieve such a feat while he was alive.

Aware that even Elvis fans could eventually have too much of a good thing, the double album's 23 tracks included eight songs that he had never recorded before. Among the highlights were 'Something' by The Beatles, James Taylor's funky 'Steamroller Blues', Frank Sinatra's 'My Way', Roy Orbison's 'It's Over' and a couple of covers to remind long-term fans of Elvis' country roots – Jim Reeves' 'Welcome To My World' and Hank Williams' 'I'm So Lonesome I Could Cry'.

As Elvis quit the stage in Honolulu early on the morning of 14 January 1973, he left as a king. Guitarist James Burton remembered Elvis being particularly buoyant after the Hawaiian show – he was still every inch the lithe, tanned, in-control king of rock'n'roll. But over the next four years, away from the bright lights, the shadows began to close in.

'ALL THE ARRANGEMENTS WERE WORKED OUT IN THE STUDIO AND EVERYTHING WAS SPONTANEOUS. TODAY EVERYBODY MAKES RECORDS LIKE THAT BUT BACK THEN, ELVIS WAS THE ONLY ONE'

Bones Howe, producer

WAY DOWN

Written by Layng Martine

Recorded 29 October 1976 at Graceland, Memphis

Guitar: James Burton, John Wilkinson, Chip Young, Charlie Hodge
Bass: Jerry Scheff
Drums: Ronnie Tutt
Piano: Tony Brown, David Briggs
Moog Synthesizer: Shane Keister
Vocals: J.D. Sumner & The Stamps, Kathy Westmoreland, Myrna Smith, Sherrill Nielsen

Released 6 June 1977

Way Down

Following his return to the concert stage, Elvis continued performing throughout the 70s, racking up a total of more than a thousand shows. At the beginning he was energised by the re-forging of a bond with his audience. As the shows gathered momentum, Elvis drew fresh energy from his hand-picked musicians; and once settled into a groove, there was still enjoyment to be had in shuffling his show and adding new songs. Even the various venues presented fresh challenges, from the cloistered rooms of Las Vegas to the vastness of the Houston Astrodome.

Inevitably though, midway through the 70s Elvis plainly became bored with the whole thing. For twenty years he had deferred to the arrangements made by his manager on his behalf. But, having finally escaped the tyranny of Hollywood, Elvis now started to feel that his relentless touring itinerary was equally unsatisfactory.

For years he had wanted to perform in Europe. The Colonel said no. Now Barbra Streisand approached Elvis directly, asking him to co-star in her update of *A Star Is Born*. The Colonel said no. Elvis wanted to produce an action karate movie. The Colonel said no. Elvis wanted to lighten the touring schedule. The Colonel said no.

Eventually something snapped and Elvis confronted his manager demanding to end their partnership. Fine, said the Colonel, once you've paid me the money you owe me. On receipt of the Colonel's claim for the outstanding amounts due to him, Elvis had no choice but to back down. Elvis' father Vernon was particularly stunned by the parlous state of the Presley finances.

Just why Colonel Parker should have kept Elvis playing Las Vegas again and again and again remained a mystery, until it transpired that the Colonel was virtually addicted to gambling, and could swiftly translate his percentage of Elvis' earnings into winnings or – more frequently – losses on the 24-hour-a-day Vegas tables. So the show went on. And on. And on.

Elvis had revelled in the sheer scale of the satellite show from Hawaii – playing to the largest audience in the world was obviously appealing, even to someone as successful as Elvis Presley. But the years that followed marked a sad, slow and inexorable decline. At first it was just rumours, percolating out from behind the close-knit security of the Memphis Mafia. But eventually even Elvis' most loyal fans grew disturbed by what they could see happening to their beloved idol before their very eyes.

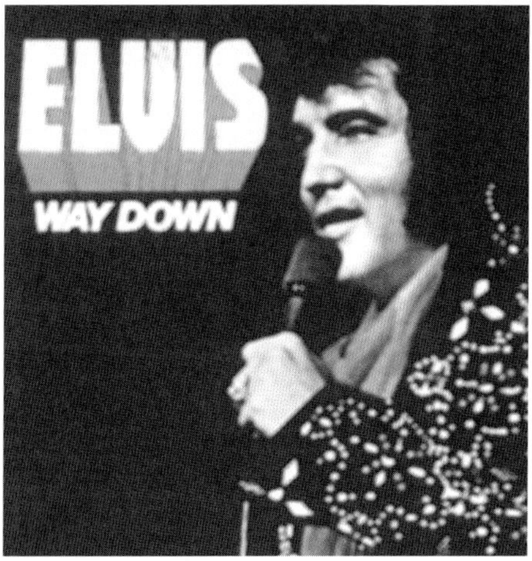

The picture sleeve featuring Elvis in a black jumpsuit, for the US release of 'Way Down'.

As Elvis' on-stage behaviour became increasingly erratic, even the Colonel grew concerned. Usually just the sight of Elvis on stage was enough for fans who had waited a lifetime for this moment; they ecstatic just to be in the same room as him. They lapped up the little stories he would tell between the songs, the self-mocking references, the irreverent asides. But gradually, as the 70s progressed, Elvis' on-stage monologues took on a far darker and more surreal edge.

On the last night of his September 1974 engagement at the Las Vegas Hilton, Elvis bombarded the baffled audience with an angry, rambling monologue about the state of his health. He had been hospitalised in Memphis towards the end of the previous year, probably as the result of a reaction to the cocktail of pills he now took on a regular basis. A year later, he was ranting on stage about newspaper reports of his drug intake. Ex-wife Priscilla who was in the audience, was shocked by such uncharacteristic behaviour. Elvis was fast spinning out of control.

During his lifetime, Elvis was never compared to rock'n'roll hedonists such as Keith Richards, Janis Joplin or Jim Morrison. His excesses were taken to be financial: he was generous to a fault, frequently handing over brand new Cadillacs to complete strangers, or donating funds to people who were down on their luck.

The rock'n'roll lifestyle was already synonymous with drug abuse: by 1973, as well as the aforementioned Jim and Janis, Jimi Hendrix and Gram Parsons had also succumbed to drug-related deaths. Marijuana, LSD, cocaine and heroin was the usual route – but although Elvis was known to have tried smoking marijuana and had taken at least one acid trip, he was also known as an outspoken critic of illegal drugs.

As it happened, most of the drugs Elvis was pumping into himself were prescribed by a doctor, and to his mind that meant they weren't really drugs at all. In the first eight months of 1977, Dr George Nichopolous had personally prescribed 5,300 pills to his patient. That's at least 25 pills every day – predominantly amphetamines, Quaaludes, tuinol, nembutal and codeine. And those are only the ones that were known about.

For a long while, rumour had it that Elvis' drug habit dated back to his days at Sun Records – when, it was suggested, he had become addicted to his mother's diet pills. But ironically, it now seems more likely that his real problem with drugs began while serving with the US Army. Allegedly, one particular platoon sergeant supplied his men with amphetamines to keep them awake and alert during all-night exercises – and amongst his troop was one PFC Elvis Presley.

The roots of his problem may have stretched way back, but Elvis' drug intake clearly did not become a real problem until his return to live performing, when the constant grind of touring saw his habit escalate. Insiders have told how Elvis needed pills to get up, and pills to put him to sleep. Pills to help him perform, and pills to help him relax.

Looking overweight but happy, the King in action, circa 1976.

Pills to wire him up, and pills to let him unwind. It was an increasingly vicious spiral.

The full extent of Elvis Presley's drug habit was kept secret from fans until very near the end. And friends, employees, family and management could only watch in horror as he visibly declined. Like so many addicts, Elvis couldn't admit he had a problem. He believed he was still in control and managing to keep up appearances, but by now the problem was too big to hide, and night after terrible night, it was spilling out on to the concert stage.

Unperturbed by the sight of his protégé disintegrating before his eyes, the Colonel continued coming up with itineraries to bring in the

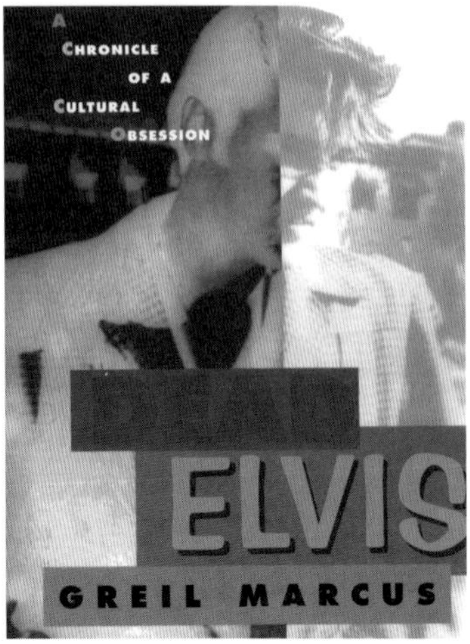

The jacket of Greil Marcus' brilliant book on the life of Elvis after his death.

bucks. During 1975 the Elvis caravan rolled through Mobile, Macon, Atlanta, Tuscaloosa, Shreveport … and half a hundred more. And each gig was slightly more desultory than the one before.

Reviewers began to single out the singer's increasing girth and lacklustre delivery. Even the musicians were concerned that he was spending more time talking to them than to his devoted fans. The quirky on-stage chats became increasingly disjointed monologues, as Elvis fell apart in full view of his audience. He now virtually sleepwalked through the 60-minute performance and fans reported a glazed, groggy performer who on occasion seemed genuinely confused about where – or even who – he was.

It wasn't just the medication. Elvis' diet was also a cause for concern. The poor Southern dishes he still favoured were a nutritionist's nightmare. Along with the deep-fried bacon and peanut butter sandwiches, a steady diet of hamburgers and candy bars, they conspired to give Elvis an unhealthy, bloated look in his latter days.

But it was the pills that were killing him. Away from touring, Elvis would simply hibernate at Graceland, his body now barely capable of functioning. He was revered and deified, but gradually over the years, Elvis had lost touch with the world outside. Pumped full of pills that plainly affected his judgement, he ended his life surrounded by sycophants telling him only what he wanted to hear.

However much of a parody he may have become towards the end of his life, Elvis Presley never lost the ability to inspire real fanaticism in his fans. Such was Bruce Springsteen's fervour, that one night in 1976 after he'd played a sell-out show in Memphis, Bruce tried to break into Graceland to give Elvis a song he'd written for him. He was politely escorted off the premises.

Springsteen wasn't the only one keen to write a hit for Elvis. In Britain alone David Bowie, Paul McCartney, Dave Edmunds, Roy Wood and Nick Lowe all had songs that would have been perfect for Elvis to record. After meeting the King in Las Vegas, Led Zeppelin – then the world's biggest rock'n'roll band – offered to back him on any selection of songs he wished to record. Of course, it never happened. Instead, the familiar material was endlessly recycled.

The release of the spoken-word *Having Fun With Elvis On Stage* in 1974 marked the nadir of a recording career that was in freefall – but still, some things never changed. His health may have been failing, his performances perfunctory, his touring schedule compounding his reluctance to enter a recording studio, but Elvis fans still demanded more Elvis music.

And, just occasionally, Elvis was capable of rising to the challenge. While his later shows were mostly pale shadows of former glories, there were still some extraordinary moments. He may have reached rock bottom, but even towards the very end, Elvis was briefly able to rekindle the fire he had first ignited twenty years before. Film footage of his final tours shows a bloated middle-aged man, but beneath all the fat, the pure beauty of a young man who had transfixed the world was just about discernible.

And then there was the one thing that never let him down – his voice. Elvis could still let rip on the big

The A–Z of Elvis

Z is for Zarathustra

Richard Strauss' tone poem 'Also Sprach Zarathustra' (a.k.a. Thus Spoke Zarathustra) became the signature tune for the opening of Elvis' live performances in 1971, after which it became permanently linked to the King. Written as a musical version of Frederick Nietzsche's poem of the same name, it is thus a musical salute to the development of the ideal of the human superman. Or, if you're Elvis, it's the neat music in that great movie, *2001: A Space Odyssey*. Which is, sadly, a more likely reason why the King chose it as the signifier for his impending entrance on stage. Dressed in his cape and spangly superman outfit he clearly needed a fittingly heroic herald to enter on. Richard Strauss provided it. After Elvis, various pop and electronica acts recorded the tune, the first being The Ventures and The Cecil Holmes Soulful Sounds, back in 1973. It was also recorded by Tomita, of course.

ballads or on gospel favourites that inspired him. Occasionally, he would sit down at the piano and perform solo – haunting, soaring, searing versions of 'You'll Never Walk Alone' or 'Unchained Melody'.

On 26 June 1977, prior to taking the stage at the Market Square Arena in Indianapolis, Elvis was presented with a plaque commemorating the pressing of his two *billionth* record. The show that night was generally agreed to be one of the best in recent memory. An uncharacteristically long 80-minute set included impassioned performances of 'Hurt' and 'Bridge Over Troubled Water' and the show was further marked out as special when Elvis invited his father Vernon to join him on-stage. But that night's show was destined to enter the history books for an altogether sadder reason: it was the last concert Elvis Presley would ever give.

'HE WAS GOOD. HE NEVER HAD TO TAKE A BACK SEAT TO ANYBODY'

Jerry Lee Lewis

As the Presley caravan careered across America during its bicentennial year, it was clear that no one was getting any real satisfaction from the experience.

Elvis had not entered a recording studio since March 1975 and his record company was concerned at the lack of new product. The fans' initial thrill at having a 'live' Elvis album had long since dissipated – what everyone needed now was Elvis singing some new songs.

Well, reasoned the record company, if Mohammed won't come to the mountain ... There had been talk as far back as 1962 of installing a recording facility at Graceland for Elvis' convenience. By 1976 that had clearly become a desperate necessity.

The first Graceland session, in February that year, did produce one bona-fide hit single in 'Moody Blue', as well as impassioned performances of 'Hurt', originally recorded by an early Elvis singing idol, Roy Hamilton; 'The Last Farewell', Roger Whittaker's sentimental hit with which Elvis became obsessed; the traditional 'Danny Boy', a favourite of Vernon Presley; and Neil Sedaka's 'Solitaire'. But the song that would take Elvis to No.1 for one last time in the 70s was not teased out of him until the final Graceland session in October 1976.

Jacket of Albert Goldman's exposé of Elvis' last day on earth. 1991.

'Way Down' is not quite 'Elvis Goes Disco', but the predominant sound is that of Shane Keister's overdubbed Moog synthesiser. The reliable Ronnie Tutt drums the song along, making 'Way Down' a convincing enough late-period Elvis single. Listening to it today, knowing what we now know about the state of his health, the energy level seems surprisingly high. Elvis' vocal may verge on the workmanlike, and the voice you really remember is J.D. Sumner's bass, going way, way down.

'Way Down' is probably not the epitaph Elvis Presley would have wished for. But then he would not be remembered solely for 'Way Down' any more than John Lennon is for 'Starting Over' – it just happened to be the record on release when he died.

Released in June, 'Way Down' was already on its way to becoming another modest hit for Elvis, when the news arrived from Memphis: Elvis had gone to the bathroom on the afternoon of 16 August 1977. And he never came back.

A LITTLE LESS CONVERSATION

Written by Billy Strange, Mac Davis
Recorded 11 March 1968, MGM Sound Studios, Culver City, California

Guitar: Scotty Moore
Drums: D.J. Fontana
Bass: Bob Moore
Piano: Floyd Cramer

Released 3 September 1968
Re-released 10 June 2002

Live A Little, Love A Little is not remembered as one of the great Elvis Presley films – in fact, for more than 30 years it was hardly remembered at all. The 1968 film was deemed to be so bad that it failed to get a British release and lay undisturbed in the vaults until early in the 21st Century …

Obscure though it was, hidden away with the film was a song that would eventually emerge from the shadows. It was originally heard on the soundtrack in a scene in which Elvis meets a 'hippy chick' at a party. Initially she resists his attentions because their star signs are not compatible, but in the best Hollywood tradition, Elvis swiftly overcomes this problem by kissing her. This liberty-taking provokes the surprised response: 'You don't taste bad for a Sagittarius'. Cue the song, 'A Little Less Conversation'.

Because only four songs had been recorded for the film there was not even a soundtrack album for fans to buy, so at the time the only place 'A Little Less Conversation' appeared was on a single. When this was released towards the end of 1968, it sank without trace on both sides of the Atlantic.

'A Little Less Conversation' had come to the film's musical director, Billy Strange, courtesy of his protégé, Mac Davis. And despite the failure of the single, Elvis was sufficiently impressed by Davis'

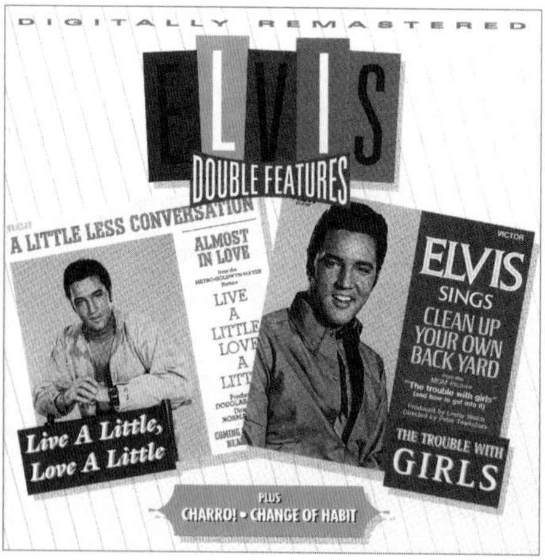

The original mix of 'A Little Less Conversation' is available on this four-film soundtrack CD release.

writing to record two more of his songs the following year. But while 'In The Ghetto' and 'Don't Cry Daddy' both became million-selling Top Ten hits for Elvis, 'A Little Less Conversation' was destined to remain stuck in limbo for over three decades.

It was the song's revival in the star-studded 2002 remake of the Rat Pack movie *Ocean's Eleven* that first alerted modern-day audiences to 'A Little Less Conversation'. Then, somewhere along the line, the song was hijacked from the soundtrack by a DJ who started scratching it around the clubs, and bit by bit, the song began to gain a cult following. But it was Nike who really brought 'A Little Less Conversation' to the world.

In anticipation of the 2002 World Cup, the sportswear company wanted something special to put in cinemas and on TV. The $90-million 'Secret Tournament' adverts, featuring world-class soccer stars and the updated Elvis track, premiered on 4 April 2002. In the usual hyperbolic ad-speak the campaign promised to 'deliver Elvis to a younger demographic in an unexpected and credible way'.

'A Little Less Conversation' had been selected from a shortlist of 300 titles, but obviously Nike couldn't just use the song as it was heard in a long-forgotten Elvis film and on the soundtrack of *Ocean's Eleven*. And so it came about that 'A Little Less Conversation' became the first Elvis track ever to be remixed with the official sanction of the Elvis Presley Estate.

Given that it was a Dutchman who made it all happen for the King in the first place – albeit one masquerading as an all-American gent called Colonel Tom Parker – it seems fitting that another Dutchman should have given Elvis what may well be his last ever No.1.

The man who deserves the credit for the controversial new version, DJ Tom Hokenburg, usually works under the name Junkie XL; but, as he explained, on this occasion he shortened it to JXL: 'Junkie is my nickname. My friends gave it to me because I used to spend so much time in the recording studio. But Elvis' estate did not want any connection with the word junkie, so I respected their wishes. It's weird to think I could be responsible for Elvis making chart history.'

It all worked better than anyone had dared to imagine it might. The momentum of the Nike advertisement, coupled with England's unexpected success in the soccer tournament, meant there was already a buzz surrounding the song when it was released as a single in the UK on 10 June. Industry insiders were still tipping Kylie Minogue's 'Love At First Sight' as a shoe-in for No.1, but within hours it became obvious who the victor was going to be, with Elvis outselling Kylie by three to one.

The record went on to sell an astonishing 250,000 copies in its first week – and suddenly, from being a song known only to Elvis aficionados, 'A Little Less Conversation' was everywhere – even on a BBC trailer promoting a Jane Austen serialisation.

Had he lived, Elvis would now be 67 years old, but this most recent hit puts Presley streets ahead of any of his younger chart rivals. To put his achievement into perspective, take all the hits by Madonna, The Spice Girls, Boyzone, Westlife, Steps and Robbie Williams, add them together – and you would still be well short of Elvis' record-breaking total of 133 British chart hits.

When it comes to No.1 singles, his only rivals are The Beatles. For the past 25 years, ever since Elvis' tragically early death propelled 'Way Down' to the top of the charts, the two acts have tied with seventeen UK No.1s apiece. In mid-1990s, with the release of two new Beatles singles, it looked as though the Fab Four might finally grab the title away from the King, but when both 'Free As A Bird' and 'Real Love' failed to reach No.1, it seemed a safe bet that the two acts' struggle for chart supremacy would remain deadlocked for all time.

Now, with his eighteenth No.1, Elvis has proved once and for all that his position as king of rock'n'roll is unassailable. 'A Little Less Conversation' has also given Elvis another place in chart history: the longest ever span of No.1 hits – just a few weeks short of 45 years between 'All Shook Up' in 1957 and 'A Little Less Conversation' in 2002.

It is an incredible and unrepeatable span. The world in which Elvis had his first No.1 would be hard pressed to recognise the 21st-century pop landscape. Initially perceived as a threat to Western civilisation, by the time 'A Little Less Conversation' reached No.1, rock'n'roll had become an integral part of the establishment it had once threatened.

The week 'A Little Less Conversation' became the UK's No.1 single was also the week Mick Jagger confirmed that, yes, he would accept the knighthood that Prime Minister Tony Blair's government had offered him. Well bless my soul.

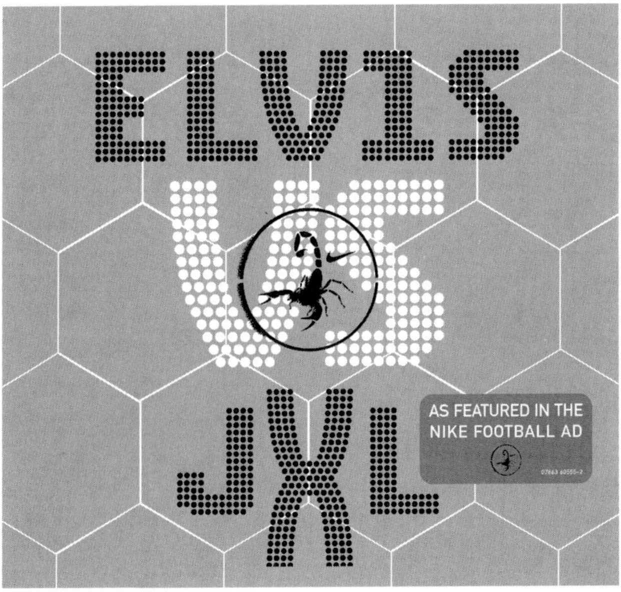

The sleeve artwork of the single that gave Elvis the all-time record of No.1 hits in the UK.

CODA

It was raining that night in 1977. I was sitting in a leaky transit van in West Norwood with the radio on. It must have been midnight when a BBC newsreader announced that Elvis Presley – 'the king of rock'n'roll' as he helpfully reminded us – had died in his Memphis home, aged 42.

I couldn't believe it. I could not believe that Elvis – *Elvis*! – was dead. Of course, at the time we were all excited and invigorated by punk, and I knew that Sex Pistols' singles and gigs by The Clash were what really mattered in rock'n'roll during that summer of 1977. Not Elvis. Elvis had ceased mattering a long time before.

But that short, sober announcement meant that we would now never see Elvis Live At Earl's Court; and that all the rumours of Elvis recording an album with The Beatles or Led Zeppelin would come to naught. For my generation, the news carried as much of an impact as the news fourteen years before of Kennedy's assassination. It was a line drawn in the sand. This really was the end of an era.

That week's music press was all over the imposter. Elvis Costello's debut album *My Aim Is True* was released in late July 1977, and ads for it were in all the inkies when Elvis Presley died in Memphis. It was good timing for Costello (although both the *Daily Mail* and *Daily Express* cancelled interviews out of 'respect').

But the old Elvis was not that easily replaced. The *New Musical Express* issue with Presley's obituary had a shot of the Memphis Flash from the 50s occupying the whole front page, with a headline insisting: 'Remember Him *This* Way.'

Once the news was out, RCA's pressing plants simply could not cope with the demand for Presley product. 'Way Down' went to No.1 in the UK and stayed there for five weeks. Within a month of his death, it was joined in the UK Top 50 by no fewer than eight reissues of classic Elvis Presley singles.

The world was in shock. Fans mourned. But Colonel Parker remained unperturbed. 'This changes nothing,' he stated immediately after being informed of his only client's death. And, once again, the Colonel was right.

Elvis has enjoyed chart hits spanning over a period of nearly five decades; he has had more No.1 hits in Britain and more weeks in the No.1 slot than any other solo act; and – with Cliff Richard hard at his heels – he has enjoyed more hits and more weeks on the British charts than any other act. In America too, chart statistics give Elvis an unassailable position: at the end of the 20th century, he was proclaimed the artist with most charted singles; he was also the artist with the most Top 10 singles; and his position as the artist who has spent the most weeks at No.1 is unlikely ever to be beaten.

In the immediate aftermath of Elvis' death, the world reeled under a deluge of tawdry memoirs, cash-in tributes and hastily compiled reissues. And over the years since, Elvis has grown into a fully fledged icon – a larger-than-life figure. But even now, the music that made him special, that made him matter so very much, is all too frequently overlooked.

There have been some honourable exceptions – Roy Carr's lovingly compiled album *The Sun Sessions* and Lee Simmonds in RCA's London office, who fought a rearguard action in the wake of Albert Goldman's character assassination. But it was the pioneering work of Roger Semon and Ernst Mikael Jorgensen – die-hard devotees who valiantly put the Elvis back-catalogue into some sort of sequence – that proved categorically, and solely on the basis of musical merit, that Elvis Presley truly deserved all the plaudits that had been lavished on him.

More recently, thanks to sympathetic biographer Peter Guralnick, Elvis has been restored as the single most important post-war cultural icon. You want to argue? Without Elvis there would have been no Beatles; no Bob Dylan; no rock'n'roll. Without Elvis: no cultural climate for the work of – deep breath – Don DeLillo, Martin Scorsese, Thomas Pynchon,

Francis Ford Coppola, Tom Wolfe ... the list is as long as that of Elvis' gold records.

Of course, the story of Elvis Presley did not end on that fateful August day in 1977. Sightings of the King continued unabated, including a rare and unconfirmed appearance on the moon. Elvis impersonators flourished, most recreating the caped and jumpsuited look of the Vegas years.

Then Elvis started appearing in the auction houses: his army duffle bag sold for £9,000; the gold pendant worn during the meeting with President Nixon went for £4,200; a Sun 78 of 'Mystery Train', £1,100; the bible Elvis gave to his grandma in 1957, £3,450. And in 1992, Elvis Presley received the ultimate accolade – his very own auction. In London and Las Vegas more than a thousand items went under the hammer, including Elvis' American Express card, birth certificate and wedding ring.

In 1982 Graceland opened its gates to the public. In 1988 Elvis was first heard advertising products on TV – when 'Stuck On You' was used in a glue ad. In 1989 a long-lost Sun acetate from 1953 – the earliest known Elvis recording – surfaced in the hands of a Memphis neighbour. In 1993 the Elvis stamp went on sale. And finally, in an act of pure millennial madness, 'Elvis 2000 – The King Returns' was officially ratified as being 'the first live tour starring a performer who is no longer living'. While Elvis was projected on to an enormous screen, musicians such as The Jordanaires and guitarist James Burton played live on stage, accompanying the virtual-Elvis who loomed above them.

In song too, Elvis lives on. The year Elvis died, The Clash had roared 'no Elvis, Beatles or Stones in 1977!' But within weeks of his death, Danny Mirror had a hit with 'I Remember Elvis Presley' and a decade later the title track of Paul Simon's 1987 album *Graceland* was a contemplation about the King's home. Tributes ranged from Dire Straits, who were 'Calling Elvis', and Marc Cohn's 'Walking In Memphis', reflecting on Elvis' home town, to the plain bizarre – Was (Not Was) released 'Elvis' Rolls

Royce', complete with a guest vocal from Leonard Cohen. The King has also been namechecked on disc by Bruce Springsteen, Cher, Eurythmics, Billy Joel, Counting Crows, Tom Petty and Van Morrison.

For U2, it was 'Elvis Presley In America', which appeared on their 1984 *Unforgettable Fire* album. In 1992 REM, then 'the world's biggest rock band' according to *Rolling Stone*, gave us their take on Elvis with 'Man In The Moon' from *Automatic For The People*. Lighter-hearted tributes came with Kirsty MacColl's 'There's A Guy Works Down The Chip Shop Swears He's Elvis' – although my favourite was Peter Singh's 'Elvis, I'm On The Phone' – was this Welsh Pakistani Elvis impersonator's album *Turbans Over Memphis* ever released?

In the end though, it is the music of Elvis Presley himself that draws you back. Again and again and again. The volatile, incandescent rock'n'roll of the mid-50s. The reflective ballads from the early 60s' films. The confident return and the triumphant stage shows of the early 70s ... there is an Elvis for everyone. Unique and irreplaceable. Unassailable as the king of rock'n'roll. And so much more, to so many people.

There is a terrible tragedy at the end of the story of Elvis Presley: you look at the itineraries and listen to the records from the 50s, when Elvis was so young and full of promise, tearing round the nation causing riots, hurling himself with abandon into live performance, and ripping it up on record. Then look at the list from the 70s, and the accounts of an overweight and listless Elvis, trundling through sets that plainly bored him and risked alienating even his loyal audiences. But it is an American tragedy, born of triumph. And *what* a triumph.

Elvis died on 16 August 1977, but he lives on in the hearts and memories of the millions who bought those records. His musical legacy was, and remains, the very foundation of rock'n'roll.

BIBLIOGRAPHY

Only Hitler and Jesus have had as much written about them as the Memphis Flash. The following titles were particularly useful on the long journey from Tupelo to Graceland.

All About Elvis
Fred L. Worth & Steve D. Tamerius (Bantam, 1981)

The Billboard Book Of Number One Hits, 4th edition
Fred Bronson (Billboard Books, 1997)

The Billboard Book Of Top 40 Hits, 7th edition
Edited by Joel Whitburn (Billboard Books, 2000)

British Hit Singles, 15th edition
Edited by David Roberts (Guinness, 2002)

Careless Love: The Unmaking Of Elvis Presley
Peter Guralnick (Little Brown, 1999)

Elvis: Day By Day
Peter Guralnick & Ernst Jorgensen (Ballantine, 1999)

Elvis: The Complete Illustrated Record
Roy Carr & Mick Farren (Plexus, 1982)

Elvis: The Hollywood Years
David Bret (Robson, 2002)

The Guinness Book Of Number One Hits, 3rd Edition
Paul Gambaccini, Tim Rice, Jonathan Rice (Guinness, 1994)

Last Train To Memphis: The Rise Of Elvis Presley
Peter Guralnick (Little Brown, 1994)